DISMANTLING
THE MYTHS

DISMANTLING THE MYTHS

FRANK MOORE

Beacon Hill Press of Kansas City
Kansas City, Missouri

ISBN 083-411-6790

Printed in the
United States of America

Cover Design: Paul Franitza

All Scripture quotations not otherwise designated are from the *Holy Bible, New International Version*® (NIV®). Copyright © 1973, 1978, 1984 by International Bible Society. Used by permission of Zondervan Publishing House. All rights reserved.
Scripture quotation marked KJV is from the King James Version.

Library of Congress Cataloging-in-Publication Data
Moore, Frank, 1951-
    Dismantling the myths : realigning moral choices with faith / Frank Moore
        p.   cm.
    Includes bibliographical references.
    ISBN 0-8341-1679-0 (pbk.)
    1. Christian ethics—Church of the Nazarene authors.   2. Decision-making—Religious aspects—Christianity.   3. Generation X.   4. Baby boom generation.   5. United States—Moral conditions.   6. Church of the Nazarene—Doctrines.   7. Holiness churches—Doctrines.
    I. Title.
    BJ1241.M66   1997
    241'.04799—dc21   ·   97-16703
                                                                    CIP

10   9   8   7   6   5   4   3   2

To
my best friend
and
companion for life,
Sue

CONTENTS

FOREWORD

In a day when we find ourselves battered around by various winds of doctrine, it is comforting to have a secure sense of direction. Frank Moore emerges from the confusion of our times with a sane interpretation of current trends in contemporary thought.

We are all philosophers. No one escapes the necessity of philosophical thought. The question is *"Who* or *what* is shaping our thought for us?"* We are coming to conclusions about everything from late-term abortions to slave labor in garment sweatshops. What basis do we use for our conclusions? Perhaps our own subjective feelings will dictate our decisions, or maybe the last book we read will provide sufficient grounds for our conclusions. But is there an objective system of thought? Is there a system of analysis outside ourselves that can be relied on to bring us to truth? Is there, in fact, a moral compass that can be relied on—one that accommodates changing times without compromising timeless truth? Frank Moore leads us through the swamp of many empty ethical systems and brings us to high moral ground. His conclusions rest on the eternal Rock tested by time and eternity.

You as a reader of this worthy book will be gratified for the time invested. Not only will you learn how to stand firm in uncertain times, but also you will discover why it is so essential to have sound answers to today's difficult questions. This is a day of great potential and unprecedented opportunity. Those with prepared minds will make the most of it.

In a world searching for identity and coherence, often the hunt is futile. Nothing makes sense. There doesn't seem to be a unifying theme. Consequently, there is an unhappy mixture of cynicism and despair. This volume penetrates the darkness with rational light and harmonizes societal discord by offering verifiable truth in easily understood concepts.

There are answers to the great issues and complexities of life. There are proven and trustworthy strategies for dealing with even a post-Christian society. The following pages do not offer easy answers to a world in quest of truth, but they do offer the right answers, tested in the crucible of time and workable for all generations. The author brings us pleasant relief from the doomsayers by providing a positive and proven handbook of standards and procedures that not only make good sense but also are founded on God's Word. His conclusions are mined from ancient thought translated into a contemporary and readily understandable format.

I have known this author for many years: first as a student, then as a university professor and as a board member of the church I pastored over those years. I realize he lives what he writes. His integrity is above reproach. He has successfully faced our contemporary ethical dilemma through soul-searching and intellectual rigor. He is a Wesleyan scholar and, more important, an authentic disciple. I am pleased to commend the man and his message for your thoughtful consideration.

—Paul G. Cunningham
General Superintendent
Church of the Nazarene

1

Getting Started

Setting the Stage

One Fateful Day

This book began in my mind nearly 12 years ago. At that time I was embarking on a new career: university professor. I had just completed several years of graduate school. Now it was time to get a real job and start paying off school bills.

Like many young professors, I had idealistic notions of my role as a university professor. Students would rush to class starving for knowledge, and I would set an inviting banquet of information on the table before them. They would eat until they had their fill and leave class contented, yet hungering for more knowledge, which I would give them at the next class session. My idealistic bubble burst the first semester in the classroom when students raised their hands and asked questions like "Do we really have to learn this?" "Who cares what Augustine said anyway?" and the most dreaded question a professor is ever asked: "Is this going to be on the test?"

Students, I soon learned, not only can challenge what you offer them but also can be brutally honest. That brings me to my motivation for writing. I remember the details of a particularly fateful day as clearly as if it were yesterday. I was waxing eloquent in ethics class about the importance of Christians making careful and wise choices regarding their personal entertainment—choices about the television programs we watch, the videotapes we check out, and the compact discs we play. The arguments sounded watertight and irrefutable to me.

Then it happened. A young lady sitting on the last row of the right section of the lecture hall raised her hand. I motioned for her to speak. She said, "I hear what you are saying, Prof, but

I don't agree. What I watch doesn't matter. In fact, I watch anything I good and well please. I'll admit a lot of it is not good, but so what? It doesn't have any effect on me. What I choose for entertainment is nobody's business but mine."

I was shocked. That girl could not have jarred me any more if she had thrown a hand grenade at my feet. I was so taken off guard by her comments that I dismissed class early that day and retreated to my office. Once safely behind the protective custody of my office door, I began to reflect; the emotional dam broke. "Why am I a professor anyway? My students are not paying any attention to what I say. Am I *that* out of touch regarding Christian entertainment choices? Maybe she's right. Maybe it doesn't matter how we entertain ourselves. I think the culture battle is over, and the Christians have surrendered." It was a dark day indeed.

On Second Thought

I did not quit my job. I'm still "professing," and I'm still challenging university students and adults daily to make wise ethical choices. But that one student's comment sent me on a 12-year journey for some answers regarding the way our commitment to Christ plays out in our everyday lifestyle choices. If my student friend had been out in left field compared to her peers, her remarks might not have impacted me. But she was not. She was right on target. She clearly articulated what most of her peers thought and, I might add, lived.

In recent years I have given my ethics students a questionnaire regarding their entertainment choices. It is one method I use to get a reading on their thinking processes regarding ethical decision-making. The majority of them have been raised in Christian homes and have attended church regularly all of their lives. Most have made a commitment to serve Christ. Yet class after class, year after year yields the same results. Most of my students are entertaining themselves with a steady diet of whatever is being offered to them on television, via cable, at the video store, and at the movie theater. Most of my baby boomer peers report that they do the same thing: turn on the television or check out a videotape with little thought of its moral content. Like army privates going through the mess line at mealtime, we boomers and Xers hold up our tray and let secular media slop just about anything onto it. No thought, no reflection—just eat whatever is on the tray. Furthermore, my students and friends will argue until their last breath that their entertainment choices have no effect on their lives. They say it is just mindless diversion to numb the boredom.

The advertising industry is aware of this boredom and has used it to their advantage. In one particular advertisement, four teenagers are standing around trying to decide on an activity to break their boredom. The unseen announcer cuts into the commercial with a list of exotic suggestions to exhilarate their senses. He suggests climbing the Swiss Alps, skydiving, sailing the seven seas, exploring the Amazon jungle, and a host of other thrilling experiences. Their blank, unimpressed stares anticipate their reply: "Been there, done that." Of course, the announcer knows something they have not done: tried the product he is selling. Clever gimmick, all-too-realistic scene. This generation has experienced so much that they are bored with the mundane events of daily life.

If I thought for a minute that my current students are out in left field compared to their peers at state schools or in the workforce or in the local church, their views might not concern me. But they're not. They're right on target, clearly articulating what most of us in our 20s, 30s, 40s, and beyond think and do.

Unfortunately, it is not just entertainment that concerns me. Life calls for dozens of moral choices in a variety of areas each day. It is a constant exercise that requires us to have a clear understanding of what is taking place, and a personal philosophy of life that keeps our choices consistent with our religious convictions. Lining up moral choices with our faith is the purpose to which this book is dedicated. It is harder than it sounds, and it requires more conscious awareness and determination than ever before.

The Audience

I am writing primarily to the age-groups I teach—baby boomers who are returning to college, and generation X. This places the range from high school graduates through the generation in their 40s. However, people younger than 18 or older than 50 may also benefit from the observations and principles offered in this work. Directing this material to a target audience requires that we draw a composite picture of the age-groups represented. This can be a risky venture. How do you accurately portray an entire generation of people in a given culture at a particular time in history? Not everyone in a particular age-group is going to match the portrait. However, certain features of each generation do emerge, giving us handles for understanding ways of interpreting philosophies of life and lifestyle choices that characterize each particular generation.

Looking through old family albums offers an insight into this principle. I am sure that neither my grandparents, my parents, my wife and I, nor our son match every characteristic offered for each of our particular generations. Yet each of us in our own way is influenced by features of the dominant culture of our generation. Pictures of my grandparents when they were in their 20s clearly identify them as citizens of the 1930s. My parents at that same age looked like citizens of the 1950s. My wife and I *unfortunately* looked like the 1970s when we got married. Our son looks like the 1990s in his recent pictures.

How does that happen? It is a combination of hair and clothing styles, accessories like glasses and hats, and background cars and landmarks. I used to laugh at old pictures of my granddad and comment on how I would not be caught dead wearing clothing styles like his. What a nightmare the first time our teenage son rushed excitedly into the house from a shopping outing with his peers! He showed us his purchase of the "hottest new clothes." Why the nightmare? You guessed it: he was dressed exactly like my granddad in those old pictures. If fashion trends hold true to form, I'll have my revenge, however. Someday he'll see his children dress in my parents' fashions or, better yet, Sue's and my old fashions. I can't wait!

What am I saying? While none of us match every characteristic of a particular generation, such generalizations do offer insights for understanding various age-groups and social and cultural influences on those age-groups. We tend to look, sound, and live like our contemporaries. We are influenced by our times. With that observation, let's look at some characteristics of the target audiences for this book.

Baby Boomers

The older group in this audience is called the "baby boomers." Nine months after World War II ended, the largest population growth in the history of the United States began. In 1946 an all-time-high birthrate reached 3.4 million. It continued to rise until it peaked in 1957 with 4.3 million births. This surge continued until 1964. Baby boomers are now 76 million strong. This same phenomenon occurred in Australia, Canada, and New Zealand.[1] Partly because of their sheer size and partly because of their unique features, baby boomers have become the most studied generation in American history. They have been analyzed with every tool and measurement of the social sciences. Bookstores abound with the latest information on them.

Baby boomer authority Landon Y. Jones sees a common thread in the four nations from which the baby boomers arose. All were nations of hope, with natural resources, open frontiers, widespread mobility, boundless optimism, and great expectations. This generation was conceived by their parents with a sense of optimism that these children would have the best of everything. They would not suffer the want and sacrifice of the Great Depression. Victory in World War II opened the doors to a bright future. Consequently, these parents made great sacrifices to give their children more than they had in their youth. They also convinced their children that they were special.[2]

Gary Collins and Timothy Clinton describe this generation as "a multifaceted, multicolored kaleidoscope that is always changing and is never able to be described with precision."[3] This is true. However, some generalizations are possible. Compared to previous generations, baby boomers tend to be better educated; more interested in material possessions; more influenced by the media and one another; more dependent upon modern technology (computers, fax machines, cellular phones, and so on); less concerned about social conventions like dressing up for work; more concerned with low-fat, low-cholesterol diets; more concerned with exercise and physical fitness; less concerned with what older people think about them; less apt to visit a specialist than to study their problem in a self-help book; and more concerned with self-fulfillment in life.

They are the first wave of citizens of the information age. Consequently, they have grown up with the sights and sounds of the entire world coming at them every day of their lives. They are children of the television, the radio, the eight-track tape, the cassette tape, the compact disc, the computer revolution, and now the global networking of the Internet. They watched with the rest of the world as Pope John XXIII was laid to rest. Men were launched into space. Soviet Premier Nikita

Khrushchev pounded his shoe on the table of the United Nations, screaming, "We will bury you!" The Soviet Union tried to
move missiles within 90 miles of United States soil. The Beatles
from England invaded our nations and our personal lives with
their music. United States President John F. Kennedy was assassinated. The war to end poverty in the United States was initiat-
ed. Inflation slipped into our economy, and we began to accu-
mulate a national debt. The Vietnam War escalated. Civil rights
leader Martin Luther King Jr. was assassinated, followed by
United States presidential hopeful Bobby Kennedy. Hippies advocated free love and mind expansion through the use of illegal
drugs. Men walked on the moon (an event that my grandmoth-
er to her dying day vowed was staged in Hollywood). Four students were killed by National Guardsmen at Kent State University for protesting the Vietnam War. Richard Nixon resigned
from the American presidency as a result of the Watergate scandal. These are only a few of the highlights of the turbulent 1960s
and early 1970s.

Why are these events important when discussing boomers?
Because the baby boomer generation was raised under the
threat of nuclear destruction, political and social upheaval, dis-
trust of national leaders and the entire political system, economic uncertainty, and more sights, sounds, statistics, and news
bites than they could possibly assimilate into their worldview. It
was information overload of the worst sort: nothing short of a
social, political, economic, cultural, and personal explosion of
sometimes contradictory information, creating a dissonance in
their minds with which they could not adequately cope. Before
they graduated from college, something had gone horribly
wrong with their parents' "better and brighter" future they had
been promised. James Bell, student of baby boomers, says their
world "evolved from a safe, perfect, and beautiful world to a
frightening, flawed, and ugly one."[4] But life moved on, so they
took the broken pieces of their shattered worldview and made a
new one—one very different from that of their parents.

Daniel Yankelovich, contemporary sociologist who has
done extensive research on American workers, does an excellent job of characterizing this shift of worldview in his book
New Rules. He says the parents of baby boomers lived by what
he calls a giving/getting compact. Here is his summary of that
worldview:

I give hard work, loyalty and steadfastness. I swallow my frustrations and suppress my impulse to do what I would enjoy, and do what is expected of me instead. I do not put myself first; I put the needs of others ahead of my own. I give a lot, but what I get in return is worth it. I receive an ever-growing standard of living, and a family life with a devoted spouse and decent kids. Our children will take care of us in our old age if we really need it, which thank goodness we will not. I have a nice home, a good job, the respect of my friends and neighbors; a sense of accomplishment at having made something of my life. Last but not least, as an American I am proud to be a citizen of the finest country in the world.[5]

In other words, parents of baby boomers worked at jobs they often found unfulfilling to earn a good paycheck so they could meet their obligation to their family and be productive members of society. They did it without question and with a sense of pride in both their work ethic and their country.

Yankelovich contends that most boomers did not grow up to adopt their parents' ethic of self-denial or duty. Rather, because of all they had been through, they opted for an ethic of self-fulfillment. Their entire life journey is best characterized as a search for self-satisfaction in every area.[6] They have a duty, all right—a duty to self. This search for self-fulfillment is why they are often referred to as "the 'me' generation." The social and cultural upheaval of their youth marked them for a lifetime and, for a multitude of reasons, turned them inward. All these influences blended together to create a dilemma of life with which boomers have been plagued.

The way this dilemma translates into ethical decision-making for boomers will be considered in chapter 2.

Generation X

The younger group of my audience is commonly referred to as "generation X." They are the children of the baby boomers, with birth years falling roughly between 1961 and 1981. This group is 38 million strong.

Generation X is often misunderstood. Social researcher George Barna says they are "the most ignored, misunderstood, and disheartened generation our country has seen in a long time."[7] Generation X is going in so many different directions socially, politically, and religiously. While some members of this generation are very passionate about certain causes, most are not. In fact, many analysts identify them with an "X" because they say they stand for nothing and believe in nothing. Their identity is missing. Andrés Tapia, associate editor for Pacific News Service, notes that the baby boomers were ready to save the world when they were in their 20s; generation X does not feel they can save even themselves. "Survival is their goal."[8]

Generation X is also referred to as "the age of indifference." Many of them don't read newspapers or watch television news. They often don't follow current events, world leaders, or world issues. Many are politically apathetic and don't vote. Many just don't care.[9] An appropriate question could be "Will generation X even read this book if it's not required for a college course?" Perhaps the Xers who read it voluntarily are more in touch with society than their contemporaries. And perhaps many Xers will learn the truths presented in this book only through caring baby boomers who will pass it on through parenting, mentoring, or teaching.

My wife, Sue, who also teaches at my university, frequently comments about the indifference of Xers. She is often called upon by other faculty members to conduct awareness classes for students to help them become more aware of what is happening in our world. She is almost always amazed at how little awareness our students have about world situations and events. Our geography professor says entering students cannot place most countries of the world on their respective continents, or states of the United States in relationship to one another. Many of our students are simply not in tune with the outside world. This is certainly not to imply that they are lacking in intellectual ability. Rather, they simply don't see this information as important to their lives, so they don't learn it. Their attitude toward almost everything is their famous response: "Whatever." They are numb to their world around them and numb to their world within.

While this characterization might be an overstatement for an entire generation of young people, it is fair to say that they have been reluctant to adopt any common worldview or system of thought that binds them together into a cohesive unit. This is especially true for their lack of ethical commitment. William

Mahedy quotes a high school teacher's insightful remark about this generation: "There is simply no moral compass."[10]

They are the second television generation, with a new twist. Now the television is giant-screen, in color, with Dolby surround-sound stereo, a cable connection, a videocassette recorder (VCR) connection, a Sega compact disc (CD) connection, and a satellite dish connection. When I was growing up, our television antenna received three channels when properly adjusted and the weather was agreeable. Now 20 to 50 channels are the norm, with satellite dish reception adding another 100 to 200. Media prophets predict this is only the tip of the iceberg for the options of the children of generation X.

Along with television have come the personal computer revolution and its connection to the World Wide Web, "the information superhighway"—the Internet. Today with a few keystrokes from the privacy of their bedrooms, young people can access information located in any major library in the world.

A spin-off of the computer revolution has been the video game explosion. First came the big black-and-white Ping-Pong games at isolated public locations. Then came video arcades at the mall with more sights and sounds than the human mind can comprehend. But why live at the arcade? Why not bring it all home and hook it up on the family television? Although early graphics were not impressive, the latest CD versions have television-quality pictures. And that's only the beginning of the technology. Now the industry is moving rapidly into "virtual reality," which puts the consumer in the center of the action. This generation has certainly not lacked in the area of visual stimulation. The television, computer, and video game have profoundly shaped them.

Just as the baby boomers did, generation X has also had its share of social and cultural influences. They have lived through the fall of Communism almost worldwide; the Persian Gulf War; the savings and loan scandal; the spiraling of the national debt out of control into the trillions of dollars; the stock market crash of 1987; the moral failure of major television evangelists; the AIDS epidemic; corporate restructuring, with massive unemployment for many of their parents; acts of terrorism such as the bombings of airliners, the World Trade Center in New York City, the United States military base in Saudi Arabia, and the Alfred P. Murrah Federal Building in

Oklahoma City; violent gangs; drive-by shootings; MTV; *Sesame Street*; and the rapidly changing music and entertainment industry. Like their boomer parents, they have grown up with political, economic, and cultural uncertainty. A better and brighter future has not been theirs either. Social analysts often comment that, economically speaking, they are the first generation in American history who do not have hope of having it better than their parents. The runaway train of consumerism has slowed dramatically.

But culture, economics, and politics are not the whole picture. There is a personal side to this picture as well. Remember—this is the generation raised by "the 'me' generation." That is a very important piece of the puzzle. As one of my students related to me, "My parents never had time for me. They were always too busy trying to find themselves or impress their friends"—a rather insightful observation about the boomer generation. William Mahedy claims boomers are the most selfish generation in American history. He does not contend that previous generations were not selfish, but at least they masked their self-centeredness and followed through with their obligations to their families. He says generation X resents the boomers because the boomers spent so much time on self pursuits that they neglected their children.[11]

Boomers had the money to buy the latest media trinkets or video game sensation, but they often did not have time to take a personal hand in raising their children. Mahedy was a military chaplain during the Vietnam War. He is now a college chaplain and counselor. While there was little difference between the student population of his college days and the students he ministered to through the early 1980s, very shortly he began to notice a change. The next generation of students seemed troubled, more traumatized than before. In fact, they began to exhibit many of the same characteristics of soldiers injured in the Vietnam War. He calls it "posttraumatic stress disorder" (PTSD), a condition resulting from the stresses of war (combat, torture, rape, violence, death, and so on).[12]

What is it that generation X has experienced to cause them to have posttraumatic stress disorder? Pick up a newspaper or newsmagazine, and you will see sexual abuse; racial tensions and riots; a skyrocketing divorce rate, bringing about the disintegration of the family; uninvolved or disinterested parents; absentee fathers or mothers; latchkey kids; AIDS; drive-by shoot-ings; random acts of violence; rape; abductions; and a host of other contributors. Mahedy contends that it is stressful just liv-ing under current social conditions: "The present social disorder is so great that simply being young today is a stressor for a huge segment of the twentysomething [sic] generation."[13]

The Road Ahead

So these are the audiences to whom I address this work: the boomers and the Xers. I have divided the book into four sec-tions:

1. The current moral climate among baby boomers and generation X: chapter 2
2. How most people in our society think and how the cul-ture war affects us: chapters 3 and 4
3. What we believe and what the Bible says about making moral choices: chapters 5 and 6
4. Strategies for lining up our personal and community lives with our faith and relating properly to our world: chapters 7, 8, and 9

Several books have been written on this general subject. So why add another to the collection? This book is different for a variety of reasons.

1. This book is written *from a positive perspective.* So many books on this subject reflect an attitude of doom and gloom. They are often written by people at the end of their careers, looking back with remorse over how society is decaying and longing for a return to "the good old days." Other books are written with a spirit of sensationalism, for the purpose of selling books. This book will give you strategies to help solve the prob-lem rather than simply to lament a hopeless situation.

2. This book is written *for the average reader.* Many of the books on the market are written in a scholarly writing style, with a scholarly vocabulary, addressed to a scholarly audience. The content is excellent, but it is difficult to decipher. This book is written in a readable writing style. It is not intended as a scholarly commentary on culture and society, but as a helpful tool for the average college student or adult. The content has been edited to keep it short and to the point.

3. This book is written *to you.* Almost all the books on the market are written to an older generation *about* the social and

cultural crisis of today. They speak of boomers and Xers as though we are in the other room and cannot hear what is being said. No one seems to be focusing their attention on those of us caught in the middle of the moral battle who are looking for answers.

4. This book is written *for practical application*. Rather than just document the situation and make the point that we are in the biggest moral struggle of our nation's history, this work goes on to give practical, step-by-step suggestions of ways to be victorious in our daily lifestyle choices and help stem the tide of moral decay. When you finish reading this book, you will have handles on things you can do to be more consistent in your Christian lifestyle choices.

5. This book is *interactive with the reader*. It is easy in this fast-paced world to read a book quickly, taking information into our heads without applying it to our thinking or lifestyle. Research indicates that baby boomers and generation X prefer a book divided into manageable pieces with opportunity to interact. This book is divided into many sections and filled with opportunities for you to pause and think about what you have just read. If you will stop and incorporate the information into your thinking and life, it will become yours. So each time you come to *Think About It*, stop and think about it. It will be well worth your time. The last three strategy chapters offer helpful exercises for you to apply to your life.

Ethical Choices on the Road of Life

When I think of making wise ethical choices, I am reminded of an experience my family and I had last summer. Sue and I taught summer school at a Christian college in Switzerland. When our classes were completed, the college president lent us a school car for sight-seeing. One of our trips took us to Salzburg, Austria, home of Wolfgang Mozart and setting for *The Sound of Music*. In order to get there, we had to go through the Arlberg Tunnel. I have been through numerous tunnels in my travels, short ones in which I could always get to the other side fairly quickly, in which I could usually see the other side when I entered.

Not the Arlberg. Oh no. It was 8.7 miles straight through the mountain. I thought we would die in a mighty, thunderous collapse of concrete and steel before we ever saw sunlight again. Rescuers would never recover our bodies. However, we made it through safely. Once we reached the other side, I promised myself I would never do that again! We would just have to take another route on our return trip to Switzerland.

So on our way back, I convinced my family that it would be fun to go *over* the mountain this time! They compliantly agreed to my uninformed plan, and up we went. We soon discovered the reason we could not see the top of the mountain from its base: it was in the clouds! After about 50 switchback turns, *we* were in the clouds too. We were also all by ourselves up there, since everybody with sense went through the tunnel. We soon traded the warm spring air for snow and slick pavement. A few days earlier I had worried about the mountain falling in on me. Now we were about to slide right off the top! But the trip was worth the effort. The scenery was breathtakingly beautiful; words cannot capture the sights we saw that day. (The sights from just below the cloud line, that is. Above it we couldn't even see as far as our hood ornament!) It was truly a rare experience of our European vacation.

I have since thought about that mountain trek when compared to the moral choices we make every day. Our trip over Arlberg Mountain took a lot of extra effort, and we went by ourselves. But I'm glad we did it. Philosophers and writers for thousands of years have talked about seeking a less-traveled road in making wise moral choices. As Robert Frost put it, "Two roads diverged in a wood, and I—/ I took the one less traveled by, / And that has made all the difference."[14]

The Bible in Gen. 13 gives us a clear illustration of the two types of moral choices. Here we see Abraham and his nephew Lot parting ways and separating their livestock because their hired hands could not get along. Abraham allowed Lot to make the first choice for grazing land; the elder Abraham should have made the first choice, but he gave preference to his nephew. Lot selected the lowland of the Jordan plain because it appeared more fertile. Abraham took the area of Canaan that was left, an area strongly resembling a desert! It sounds like purely agricultural choices. But the Bible makes a lot more of the two choices than that. Lot's lowland became symbolic of self-seeking pleasure, because of its close proximity to the sinful cities of Sodom and Gomorrah, cities God later destroyed. Abraham's choice became symbolic of a person seeking to please God, because of Abraham's exemplary spiritual life. In fact, God made another promise to bless Abraham right after he expressed his willingness to take the leftover land (vv. 14-17).

Choices like Abraham and Lot's are still being made every day in our lives. We cannot always follow the examples of our peers or our neighbors. We cannot always accept what our society or popular culture offers us. We cannot look to see where the crowd is going. We cannot search out "greener pastures." As in the choice of Abraham, God is calling us to the less-traveled road.

What do these metaphors tell us about the road less traveled? They tell us it is often difficult

- to live counter to our culture,
- to refuse to compromise our standards,
- to live differently from our friends,
- to say no when friends invite us to participate in questionable acts,
- to stand alone,
- to be identified with the minority position,
- to resist the temptation to conform,
- to control our desires and say no to inappropriate expressions of natural appetites,
- to be called names by those who don't have the courage to join us,
- to take the name of Christ and identify with His cause.

Killing Us Softly

If you have been around the Christian community for very long, you have probably heard many of the preceding ideas. So why bring them up again? Because we are living in a new day with regard to the influence of culture on our Christian community. Culture is *killing us softly*. By that, I mean it is entirely possible for us to be so lulled to sleep by culture and desensitized to its powerful influence that we begin thinking and acting in ways that betray our religious beliefs without realizing what is happening to us.

I admit that the early chapters of this book may paint a dark picture. But it is not a hopeless cause. This is a book filled with hope for the culture battle. We as a Christian community must inform ourselves of the current situation and join the timeless battle for the hearts and minds of people. We must wake up to what is happening all around us before we can do something about it.

We sometimes complain about the fact that our society is going through tough times morally, but that's nothing new. Christians have *always* had to fight on the side of good and righteousness in a hostile and alien environment. Before we joined the battle, many other Christians fought it for almost 2,000 years, and before them the Hebrew people of the Old Testament had been championing the cause for thousands of years. It has been a constant and sometimes heated battle. Often in history Christians have shone most brightly when they were fighting the hardest for truth and righteousness. We can learn lessons from the struggle of our ancestors and can employ some of their tactics today to maintain our piety and identity as we change our world for the better.

In one of my adult classes, made up almost exclusively of baby boomers, I give an assignment in which students read the Old Testament book of Ecclesiastes, a book written nearly 3,000 years ago, and then write an analysis. They are especially looking for principles for daily living. Sometimes they grumble about the assignment, asking, "How could something written 3,000 years ago possibly speak to my situation today?" When they return to class the next week with their completed papers, they report how amazed they are at how contemporary the writer of Ecclesiastes is in addressing situations that face them in their lives today. The reason for this, of course, is because Ecclesiastes is about the human condition. Modern technology and advancements in science do not basically change human nature. Human beings have the same needs and the same general makeup today that they had 2,000 years ago (in Jesus' day), 3,000 years ago (in David and Solomon's day), or 4,000 years ago (in Abraham's day). In fact, from as far back as Adam and Eve, we learn that people are basically the same. And so, as we look to the Bible, we will be amazed at how helpful its admonitions are for us in our day of moral bankruptcy.

I'm often asked as an ethics teacher if I'm discouraged at the moral decay of our generation. While I'm concerned about the current state of affairs, I'm not discouraged. This gives the Church the opportunity to be the salt, the light, and the yeast to our needy world that God has called us to be. We shine best when our environment is darkest. This also gives us a platform from which to share the good news of Jesus Christ.

Actually I'm quite hopeful, and I offer this book in the light of that hope.

It's time to begin our study by looking at the current situation of society in general and the Christian community in particular.

2

Say "Cheese"

*Taking a Snapshot of Baby Boomers
and Generation Xers*

Off to Class

Every Tuesday and Thursday at 10:55 A.M. I put on my asbestos-lined bodysuit, boxing gloves, and baseball catcher's mask. I then pick up my lecture notes and fire extinguisher, say a brief (but desperate) prayer, and head off to ethics class. I have been standing in front of ethics classes each fall and spring semester and summer school session for more than 11 years. Fall and spring semester classes have about 80 students each; the summer session has about 15 to 20 students. The faces change each semester; that is, *most* of the time they change. Unfortunately, two or three students each semester are working too many hours, taking too many classes, or having too much fun to keep up with their classwork. These students then get a "second blessing" of ethics!

I spend the first three weeks of class presenting the philosophical theories that most people use in making ethical decisions. I show the positive and negative features of each theory. With these theories in hand, I then look to the Bible for a biblically based foundation for making ethical choices. Next, I survey the current cultural scene. I try to show students where we are as a society. For example, one of the fact sheets looks like this.

Every day in America . . .

1,000 unwed teenage girls become mothers
1,106 teenage girls get abortions

4,219 teenagers contact sexually transmitted diseases
500 adolescents begin using illegal drugs
1,000 adolescents begin drinking alcohol
135,000 kids bring guns or other weapons to school
3,610 teens are assaulted; 80 are raped; 630 are robbed
2,200 teens drop out of high school
16 teens are murdered
13 teens commit suicide[1]

I realize these statistics do not accurately represent the lives of most of my students, but they do reflect our society in general. I used to not worry. After all, the damaging effects of moral decay are happening out in the world somewhere—far beyond where I live and work. My students are basically good individuals—most of them were raised in Christian homes and have been regular attenders of Sunday School, youth group, and church, and are now students at a Christian college. I guess I also thought living in the center of the nation somehow insulated my students and me from the corroding influences of society in general.

I have since changed my mind about this assumption. In one way or another we are all impacted by our society. In time the factors that contribute to the events in the above list work their way into our lives and begin to influence our own thinking and lifestyle. So I go into class on Tuesdays and Thursdays painfully aware of the moral battle facing each of us daily.

After I present the philosophical theories, biblical foundations, and cultural survey, we discuss one ethical topic in each class session for the remainder of the semester. Students make persuasive presentations. Two students make a logical case in favor of each issue; two give the opposing viewpoint. Discussion is always lively and sometimes heated. That is when the asbestos-lined bodysuit, boxing gloves, and catcher's mask come in handy. Sometimes it seems almost like putting out a fire, breaking up a riot, or deflecting flying objects.

Even though the faces change each semester, student views of various ethical topics remain rather consistent from year to year. Occasionally we vote our personal convictions at the end of a particular ethical discussion. I can usually predict the result of the vote, based on previous semester results. I have taught this class long enough and have heard enough student responses across the years to have a fairly accurate pulse of what they are thinking and how they are living. Frankly, I'm becoming more and more troubled with what I see and hear. The philosophies for making ethical decisions and methods of reasoning are sounding more like the culture than I care to admit.

Student views have shifted significantly over the past decade. Nothing dramatic at any one time. No avalanche of eroding morality. Just a subtle shift here and there, which over time has created a substantial difference. The fact that views are changing is not surprising. After all, public opinion even among Christians is always changing. What is notable is the directional drift toward popular culture. About five years ago I awakened to the fact that the shifts were beginning to create a completely new picture.

Research surveys on both baby boomers and generation X have verified my observations. Two surveys of Christian generation Xers have played a significant role. The first was conducted with our student body a couple of years ago by the Office of Student Development at the university where Sue and I teach. They had given the same survey to the student body 11 years prior, creating a point of reference for comparing students a decade earlier. The results of the recent survey came as no surprise to me. But it did give me scientific evidence to back up what I had been observing informally in class for the past several years. A second survey was conducted by the Barna Research Group of Glendale, California. This survey was taken of 3,795 churched teens from 13 conservative, Evangelical denominations in youth group meetings from November 1993 to March 1994. The survey showed that 82 percent of the teens attend church every week, 73 percent attend weekly youth group meetings, and 67 percent are in Sunday School class every Sunday. They were clearly teens of our Christian community. Results from these surveys form the basis of the next section.

My concern as an ethics teacher is that culture is killing us softly and desensitizing us to its powerful influence. Without realizing it, we begin thinking and acting in ways that our culture suggests. I don't believe popular culture is all-powerful to the point that we cannot resist its influence. I also don't believe in determinism, which says we have no choice but to respond as culture wants us to respond, like metal shavings to a magnet. Human beings are not passive metal shavings controlled by environment. We are reasoning individuals, created in the image of God. We have the ability to make righteous choices, even in the face of the moral collapse of popular culture. Nevertheless, we must be on constant alert to the subtle tendency toward a drift in the direction of popular culture.

A Picture of Generation X

The two generation X surveys lead to some important and startling conclusions. These observations may not reflect the way all generation Xers feel and think, but they reflect the way a significant number do. Even though these surveys were taken on Xers, the findings are fairly representative of baby boomers as well. The temptation exists for an older generation to look on a younger one with a judgmental "Ain't it a shame?" mentality. That should not happen in this case, because Xers reflect attitudes prevalent in boomers as well. Thus the following observations often use inclusive language.

1. *The influence of popular culture and society in general may be far more powerful than we might realize or care to admit.* By "popular culture" I mean the music, video, movie, and television industries along with the fads and fashions we see at the mall or on the street. By "society in general" I mean the beliefs and norms that are coming to us from all sources other than home and church. We would like to think that as Christians we live our lives in one realm, and the non-Christian world lives in another. To some extent this is true. Our Christian lifestyles verify this. Our nonparticipation in the sinful practices and habits of the world is one indication that we are citizens of another realm. Furthermore, our practices of personal piety, such as prayer, Bible reading, witnessing, and Christian stewardship and service indicate that we're heading in a different direction than the world around us.

So if we're reading our Bibles, going to church, and sharing our time, money, and influence with others, and if we are not joining our friends in sinful practices, then where is the problem? This is where social and cultural influence become so subtle. Without even realizing it, we can begin to *reason* like the world. The lines between godly convictions and worldly practices become blurred in our thinking. In fact, with time we are not even sure where the lines differentiating the two are anymore. Once-black-and-white issues become various shades of gray. We know as Christians we are called by Christ to be different from the world, but we can become unsure why or how to accomplish this.

Sociologist Daniel Yankelovich observes that 80 percent of Americans are affected at the very root of their philosophy of life by shifts in culture.[2] If we choose to withdraw totally from the world and live our lives in total isolation like the monastics of the Middle Ages, we might be able to avoid much of culture's influence. However, in order to accomplish this, we would have to do more than move. We would also have to leave our television, radio, newspaper, telephone, CD player, and computer modem behind. They are all conduits of cultural influence. Withdrawal is not a very practical solution to the problem. We block the front door only to have culture's influence enter through the back. Therefore, we acknowledge that Yankelovich is right—most of us are affected by culture. A friend of mine commented recently that he and his wife made a decision when they married that they would not have a television in their home. They did not want its influence on their family. They discovered, however, that the influence of television still found its way into their family through other sources. My friend lamented, "We can't seem to avoid television's influence."

You've heard it said that "you are what you eat." It is also true that we are what entertains us and what lifestyle choices we make. We become like the things we take into our lives. If we note an inconsistency between our convictions and our choices, we do one of two things. We either correct the inconsistencies, or we adjust our convictions to fit our lifestyle. For example, when I was a child growing up on the farm, I sometimes played baseball with my two brothers and sister. I played outfield. Whenever my sister hit a fair ball into the outfield and no one was looking, I secretly moved the boundary marker to make the ball "out of bounds." (I was a very ornery brother!) In like manner, it's sometimes easier to move the ethical boundary lines to accommodate our behavior than it is to radically alter our lifestyle choices, especially if those alterations make us conspicuously different from our peers.

Culture and society have a way of affecting us even when we are not overtly surrendering to its influences. It becomes so much a part of the air we breathe that we find it difficult to avoid its subtle intrusions into our lives. We may have trouble *seeing* our culture because we so naturally see *with* our culture. Culture becomes the lens through which we view the rest of the world. That lens offers a strong influence on life.

2. *We have a good grasp of Christian beliefs as they have been passed down to us through tradition.* Some misunderstanding is occurring, based largely on the influences of culture and society. However, for the most part we have a fairly accurate head knowledge of the faith. We also have an adequate vocabulary for talking about our faith. In other words, we know the religious language of our heritage.

The survey conducted at our university questioned students' knowledge of the Christian faith with regard to God the Father, Son, and Holy Spirit; the Trinity; the inspiration and authority of Scripture; original sin; acts of sinning; salvation; the second coming of Christ; and life after death. Students did very well at making consistently accurate doctrinal statements. All indications from this survey are that we have a solid core of Christian beliefs. There is always more to learn, but most of us can make a passing grade on a basic Christian beliefs test.

The Barna survey came to the same conclusion with its high schoolers. Seventy percent believed the Bible is totally accurate in all its teachings, and they knew what those teachings are. An overwhelming majority offered correct responses with regard to basic Christian beliefs regarding God the Father, Son, and Spirit; Satan; sin and salvation; justification by grace through faith; a personal relationship with Jesus Christ; heaven and hell with eternal rewards and punishments; and the unique superiority of Christianity over the other religions of the world. Various doctrines were presented in a variety of ways to determine if students actually understood what they were saying. All indications are that they understood clearly.[3]

3. *It's easy to build a wall in our thinking between what we say with our religious language and what we live with our lives.* By this I mean we know what to say when we're at church or in a religion class at college. Our religious talk is articulate. But the lifestyle choices we make on a daily basis often betray what we say when we're in our religious mode. I'm not implying we intend to be hypocritical. We are certainly not aware of any hypocrisy. The root meaning of the word "hypocrite" is "putting on a mask." It comes from the ancient theatrical world, in

which actors held up a smiling mask when they were playing characters who were happy and a frowning mask when playing characters who were sad. They did this for the benefit of people sitting near the rear of the audience who might not be able to see their facial expressions. Hypocrites today hide behind masks while having some awareness of the inconsistencies in their lives. I don't think we have the intention of a double standard. It is more subtle than that.

We can effectively compartmentalize our lives and minds to the point that we sometimes think and live in two mutually exclusive spheres. Compartmentalism has become a standard concept in ethical textbooks. It means separating our personal world into two realms: *the sacred realm,* in which we look and act our Christian beliefs at church, school, and home; and *the secular realm,* in which we live the rest of our lives. What we think or say in our religious world does not always inform what we do in our daily lifestyle. Robert Bellah and his associates comment in *Habits of the Heart* that this is the most distinctive change of American society in the 20th century.[4] Compartmentalism usually happens subtly and involuntarily.

Our university survey showed up a serious discrepancy between what students say and what they do. For example, 92 percent of the students say they feel premarital sex is wrong in every case, yet 26 percent of them have engaged in sexual intercourse, and another 17 percent have gone beyond heavy petting and stopped just short of intercourse. That represents nearly half (43 percent) of the students surveyed. In addition, those numbers are up from the previous survey of 21.5 percent for sexual intercourse and 15 percent for stopping just short of intercourse.

The Barna survey reached the following conclusions. When asked, "What is morally acceptable for two people who are not married but are both in love and are willing?" students responded:

Fondling of breasts: 35 percent always or sometimes
Fondling of genitals: 29 percent always or sometimes
Sexual intercourse: 20 percent always or sometimes

Note how this compares with what these same high schoolers say they have already experienced with the opposite sex:

Fondling of breasts: 34 percent yes
Fondling of genitals: 26 percent yes

Sexual intercourse: 16 percent yes

The percentage points between what these teens *think* in their heads and what they *do* on their dates are not very far apart. Note 35 percent compared to 34 percent, 29 percent compared to 26 percent, and 20 percent compared to 16 percent. In other words, if they believe with their heads it is morally acceptable, they are almost certain to do it with their lives. This realization becomes frightening when we factor in their responses to the following question:

If the opportunity presented itself *today*, how likely would you be to have sexual intercourse with another person if
you were in love with the person—45 percent more likely
you really intended to marry that person—44 percent more likely[5]

Both surveys indicate a fairly solid wall between religious language and conduct.

4. *Lifestyle choices tend to be made more on the basis of individual or personal reasoning than on the thinking of the larger group, such as a youth group, local church, or denomination.* When we weigh the pros and cons of a particular choice, we tend to decide more on the basis of what we personally think and feel rather than what the larger community to which we belong thinks or feels. Not only do we not hold ourselves accountable to the larger Christian community, but also we do not have much regard for what our ancestors or those of our tradition thought and taught on these matters.

We have all had the experience as young children of asking one of our parents for permission to do something, only to have him or her deny our request. When we asked, "Why not?" we were told, "Because I told you so." What kind of an answer is that? It's an answer that indicates that parents sometimes impose their own personal value system on their children. Your request was denied simply because your parent didn't feel it was a wise choice. Case closed.

That line of reasoning does not work with baby boomers or generation X, even in the church. The corporate conscience of a larger group like a youth group, local church, or denomination carries less weight today than it did a generation ago. By corporate conscience we mean the advice that comes to us from the lessons learned by those who have gone before us on the journey of life. Some people have made bad decisions and have shouted back, "Don't come this way—it's a dead-end road." Others have made good decisions and offer their example as a good path to follow. These good and bad decisions create a fund of advice from a large number of people over a long period of time. We inherit this fund as a Christian community and call it our "corporate conscience." But this idea has fallen on hard times in recent years. We no longer seem to care as much about what the old-timers thought. The individualism that has characterized America from the early days of the pioneers and cowboys now represents the moral thinking of our day. I have only one person to answer to: *myself.* Baby boomers have exercised their right of individual personal choice more than any generation in the past[6] and have taught generation X to follow suit.

Take an example from our university survey questions regarding the use of alcoholic beverages. Although 81 percent of the students surveyed say they know their home church does not approve of the use of alcohol, 79 percent of the students do not hold that position themselves. It doesn't matter to them that the home church or youth group disapproves of this lifestyle choice—the decision to drink is made solely on the basis of personal reasoning, and most students don't have a problem with such logic.

These statistics don't mean that 79 percent of our students are social drinkers (that number is about 25 percent). They simply don't see anything wrong with it. It is the first step in breaking down their resistance to a change in their behavior. As we saw in the Barna survey in the last section, once we no longer disapprove of an action in our thinking, we become a prime candidate to participate in that action.

5. *Tolerance of opposing ethical, social, and religious positions is more acceptable.* This is partly the result of our information age. We are exposed to large quantities of facts, feelings, attitudes, and motivations on a daily basis. They come to us from the television, radio, newspaper, and so on. Much of this information offers opposing viewpoints. How do we decide between them? The most convenient response is *not* to decide. Just grant it all an equal hearing and suspend judgment. After all, tolerance and open-mindedness are major themes of our day. It is not politically correct at this point in our history to be critical of positions other than our own. So we reason, "To each his own," or

"Live and let live," and we go on our way, content to live our lives as we desire with no critical analysis of what others are doing with their lives.

Nondrinking students not having a problem with those who drink is only one example of many Christian attitudes toward a variety of social positions. As one of my colleagues put it, "Everything is up for grabs." Daniel Yankelovich illustrates how language betrays cultural values. Unmarried members of the opposite gender cohabiting was once called "living in sin." Now it has been neutralized to a more politically correct "living together." What was once deviant sexual behavior is now called "alternate lifestyle." Such changes in our cultural attitudes and language have had the effect of softening our Christian conviction on many ethical positions.[7]

I can remember class discussions 10 years ago regarding homosexuality in which most students expressed a very strong opinion in opposition to the practice (not against the persons). In fact, such discussions often required the use of my symbolic fire extinguisher to "cool off" their fiery words. Today I cannot generate a lively discussion about homosexuality in most classes. Students have seen such positive homosexual role models in the media, and they have been taught such tolerance in their high school education, that they leave the matter to individual choice. They may not choose that lifestyle for themselves, but they have nothing to say about those who do.

6. *Our list of irreducible minimums may be shrinking.* Irreducible minimums are those things we absolutely, positively will not do or say. We don't have to think them through or weigh the pros and cons; they're a black-and-white issue. We have our mind made up as soon as we determine the situation. The list includes everything from murder to stealing to taking God's name in vain. The shrinking of this list means we are absolutely certain about fewer things today. Gray now comes in a whole new variety of shades.

One of the questions that must be asked for an item still remaining on the irreducible minimum list is the reason a person does not participate in that particular lifestyle choice. For example, our university survey indicates that tobacco usage has dropped in the past decade from 20 percent usage in the previous study to 12 percent currently. That's a good trend. But why are our students not using tobacco? From their classroom comments, I know this is not due to religious convictions, but rather for health reasons. They don't want to harm their bodies. On many moral issues today, convictions are based on practical results.

As indicated earlier, the majority of students in the Barna and the university surveys were nurtured in a Christian environment—a Christian home, church services, youth group meetings, summer camp, Bible study fellowships, and so on. So where do they get these attitudes and perspectives? I think you know the answer to that question. These students were not raised in a morally protective bubble. Yes, they grew up in a Christian home and church environment, but they also grew up in a secular society.

Think About It

Look back over the six observations about this Christian generation. Think of a personal example of each from your own life or the lives of people you know.
1. Influence by culture
2. A good grasp of Christian beliefs
3. A wall between religious language and personal life
4. Choices made by personal reasoning rather than corporate conscience
5. Tolerance of opposing ethical, social, and religious positions
6. A shrinking list of irreducible minimums

A Picture of Baby Boomers

So what is secular society like these days? The best way to answer that question is to discover what people in this society believe and live at the grass roots. I am not talking about what the media or music industry offers; we will consider that later. I am talking about what schoolteachers, bank tellers, baseball coaches, the average Jane or Joe in our land personally believe. If we know that, we can accurately test the cultural soil in which our children have been planted.

The most extensive survey instrument and research endeavor on ethical beliefs and practices ever attempted in American history was conducted at the beginning of the 1990s. After working through over 200,000 survey questions from nearly 100 survey instruments, an oral survey 90 minutes in length and a written version were administered to 5,577 people throughout

every region of the United States. People were urged to be totally honest in exchange for anonymity. The results of this survey
were published in the book *The Day America Told the Truth: What
People Really Believe About Everything That Really Matters*, by
James Patterson and Peter Kim. The following are highlights of
this book, which give insight into what average citizens think
and do in their lifestyle choices. Here is a quick summation of
areas related particularly to baby boomers.

On Divine and Human Rules

It appears that most of us in this country are making up
our own rules of conduct. We are writing our own moral codes.
We are even deciding which divine laws we want to follow. Only 13 percent of the people surveyed believe in *all* of the Ten
Commandments. "There is absolutely no moral consensus in
this country as there was in the 1950s, when all our institutions
commanded more respect. Today, there is very little respect for
the law—for any kind of law."[8]

"It's the wild, wild West all over again in America, but it's
wilder and woollier this time. *You* are the law in this country.
Who says so? *You* do, partner."[9] Each one of us decides what is
right or wrong for ourselves, without reference to what divine
or civil law might say. The following is what we believe, based
on what we are doing.

The Ten Commandments of Popular Opinion
1. I don't see the point in observing the Sabbath (77%).
2. I will steal from those who won't really miss it (74%).
3. I will lie when it suits me, so long as it doesn't cause
   any real damage (64%).
4. I will drink and drive if I feel that I can handle it. I
   know my limits (56%).
5. I will cheat on my spouse—after all, given the chance,
   he or she will do the same (53%).
6. I will procrastinate at work and do absolutely nothing
   about one full day in every five. It's standard operating
   procedure (50%).
7. I will use recreational drugs (41%).
8. I will cheat on my taxes—to a point (30%).
9. I will put my lover at risk of disease. I sleep around a
   bit, but who doesn't? (31%)

10. Technically, I may have committed date rape, but I know that she wanted it (20% have been date raped).[10]

On Moral Leadership

Who are the moral leaders today? No one but us. Ninety-three percent say they and they alone decide what is right and wrong for them. Choices are made on the basis of personal reflection. Eighty-four percent say they have violated the established rules of their religion, and 81 percent say they have violated the law of the land because, in their opinion, those rules or laws were wrong. If the rules of the church or the land do not stand up in their own personal court, then they see no reason to obey them. "We are a law unto ourselves. We have made ourselves the authority over church and God. We have made ourselves the clear authority over the government. We have made ourselves the authority over laws and the police."[11]

On Lying

Lying is now a feature of the American character. We lie so much that we don't even know we are doing it anymore. Ninety-one percent lie regularly; the majority of us lie every week. These are not unintentional mistakes. They are willful, premeditated lies. The same observation I made about the reason my students choose not to smoke because of bad consequences applies here. That is, many people refrain from lying, not because they think it is morally wrong, but because they fear they might get caught. Conduct is controlled for reasons of utility rather than principle. To whom do we lie? To just about everyone. It appears that we lie the most to the people we know best—our family and friends.[12]

Researchers tell us we have more serious liars in this country right now than at any time in our history. Lying is the cultural norm. It is one thing to participate in an activity while recognizing that it is morally unacceptable. It is quite another to do it and see nothing wrong with it. The latter is clearly the case in our national attitude toward lying. Sixty-six percent of all Americans see nothing wrong with it.[13]

On Virginity

The number of people who are virgins when they marry and remain faithful until death is so small that it does not show up on statistical charts. The national average of virgins at the time of marriage is 29 percent. The reason their influence drops off the statistical charts in married life is due to marital unfaithfulness. Virginity is not a cherished virtue in our national consciousness.[14]

On Sex

We enjoy participating in sexual activity, but we're not satisfied. We want more of a good thing. "This sexual hunger leads us to places and practices the Bible and many federal and state laws explicitly tell us not to go. We could not care less. . . . Overwhelmingly, the American attitude toward sex (anything except sex with children) has become: Just do it."[15] We participate in sex wherever we can find it. Much of this sexual activity is not with a life partner but with a variety of people. Ninety-two percent of sexually active people in this country have had 10 or more lovers, with a lifetime average of 17.[16] It was predicted in the early 1980s that the AIDS epidemic would curtail this unbridled sexual activity. All research shows that this clearly is not the case. Our nation is as sexually active outside of marriage as ever.

Sexual practices often have their origins in sexual fantasies. Our national imagination is full of sexual fantasy. Many psychologists today teach the acceptability and harmlessness of sexual fantasy and urge people to practice it. They call it "personal entertainment." The researchers assumed that people's sexual fantasies were not lived out, that they left their sexual exploits in their head. They were wrong. They found that actual sexual experiences are often more fanciful than imaginary ones, which are often acted upon. "If we can dream it up, we just might do it."[17] It's not just straight sex that people dream about, either. The research showed that 20 percent of all men and women in this country have homosexual fantasies.[18]

Our culture does not place a high virtue on sexual purity, either in theory or in practice. Aldous Huxley expressed the national sentiment when he said chastity is "the most unnatural of the sexual perversions."[19] As with lying, we can justify anything we want to do, once we change the rules.

On Marriage

We are still getting married today as in the past, but we

have lost faith in the institution of marriage. That is, we no longer see marriage as a lifetime commitment to someone we love with all of our hearts. A third of the married men and women in the survey confessed that they had had at least one affair. Thirty percent were not really sure if they still loved their spouses. Only one in three gave love as the primary reason for getting married in the first place.[20]

Most people in the survey thought it was a good idea to live together before marriage. Almost half said they could think of no good reason to get married in the first place. After all, people can get sex without marriage; the majority of them do.[21] Marriage is looked upon as more trouble and a greater risk than it is worth. Forty-four percent of the people surveyed believe most marriages will end in divorce anyway. Fifty-nine percent believe in drawing up prenuptial agreements as a wise preparation in the event of divorce.[22]

On Having an Affair

Thirty-one percent of married people are having affairs, which generally last about a year. Only 28 percent of those having affairs plan to end them soon. Sixty-two percent think nothing is morally wrong with the affair they are having. How could it be wrong? Everyone is doing it.[23]

These statistics come as a surprise to most of my unmarried students. They often reflect in class their assumption that singles are the only people in the world who have to deal with sexual temptation. Obviously married people do not have to deal with it, they assume, because married people have social and religious permission to enjoy as much sexual activity as they desire with their married partner. My students are wrong. The same sexual temptations that urge the unmarried into premarital sex also urge the married into extramarital affairs. In fact, those who participate in premarital sex are more likely to have an extramarital affair than those who do not. Apparently the same permissive attitude that allowed them to have premarital sex carries over into the marriage relationship.[24]

Why do married people have affairs anyway? Love has little to do with it; it is simply a sexual fling. People participate in affairs just for excitement. Only 17 percent of men and 10 percent of women plan to leave their mates to be united with their lover.[25]

Our tendency toward unfaithfulness does not seem to be lessening any with time. Seventy-eight percent believe we are cheating more today than just 20 years ago. These people should know; many of them have been doing it![26]

On Violence and Crime

Crime is rapidly increasing in our society. Seventy-five percent of us have violated other people's private property. Sixty percent admit that they take things from work; 50 percent steal hotel and health club towels; 29 percent shoplift; 25 percent do not repay loans.[27]

Because of unreported crimes, it is believed that our crime statistics may be underestimated by as much as 600 percent.[28] Few of us feel safe anymore. It is a No. 1 concern in this country. We are becoming fearful of everyone we do not know. And it's not just strangers we fear. One of the most talked-about phenomena in recent years is date rape. This is an unanticipated crime of the worst sort. Twenty percent of the women surveyed reported that they had been raped by their dates. Is it any wonder why rape is on the increase when 42 percent of Americans confess that they have regular, violent sexual urges? Here again, we tend to act out our sexual fantasies.[29]

It has become common knowledge that the United States is the most violent industrialized nation in the world. The homicide rate among teenage males is 20 times higher in the United States than in Western Europe and 40 times higher than in Japan. We have 20 times the number of rapes committed in Japan, England, or Spain. When you compare our homicide rate to other similar developed nations, you see the startling difference:

- United States—13.9 per 100,000 people
- Canada—2.7 per 100,000
- Spain—2.0 per 100,000
- United Kingdom—0.8 per 100,000[30]

On Our Work Ethic

The Protestant work ethic that contributed to making the United States great is dead in national consciousness. The majority of workers surveyed say they spend 20 percent of their time at work doing absolutely nothing. Half regularly call in sick when they are not sick. One in six drink or use illegal drugs on the job. Only one in four say they give work their best effort. Half of the people in the survey believe you advance at work through politics and cheating rather than by working hard. Consequently, one in four expect that they will compromise their personal beliefs in order to get ahead at their job.[31]

Being lazy or political on the job is not the only, or even the worst, violation of the Protestant work ethic; we are downright unethical on the job. What are we doing that is unethical? The list is almost endless. The top contenders are stealing, lying, cheating, having sex on the job with coworkers, and falsifying documents.[32]

On Personal Qualities

With regard to questions of which moral attributes Americans have now when compared to the past, the survey showed that we perceive ourselves to be more materialistic, 60 percent; more greedy, 60 percent; more selfish, 59 percent; less religious, 56 percent; less honest, 54 percent; less moral, 54 percent; and less hardworking, 53 percent.[33] Note that this is how we feel about ourselves, not about someone else. Only we know what is in our own hearts.

Perhaps the most publicized findings of this survey had to do with how far we would go for large sums of money. Seven percent (1 in 14) said they would murder for money. The watershed amount at this time is about $2 million. Anything over that figure, and we will do it. Anything less, and we're not sure.[34]

On Community

While not an ethical issue itself, the subject of community is important for discussions in later chapters. The contributions of community play a major role in establishing and maintaining good ethical standards. Community is one of the foundations of moral responsibility. As with almost everything else we have studied, this concept has changed radically in our nation in recent years. "Community, the hometown as we have long cherished it, no longer exists. . . . There is no meaningful sense of community."[35] We no longer view ourselves as being members of a group of people to whom we are accountable and from whom we draw moral strength. We are each an island unto ourselves. We answer to no one, and we are responsible for no one. This is verified by the fact that 72 percent of all Americans do not know their next-door neighbors.[36] We come and go as we please without reference to anyone else in our world.

On God and Religion

The research findings on God and religion are especially insightful, for they set the foundation, or lack thereof, on which all morality is based. Ninety percent of the people surveyed say they believe in God. But this figure is misleading. When they think of God, we have good reason to believe, they are not thinking of a Supreme Being with the same attributes as come to your mind. Same word—different meaning. Six out of seven of these same people also say it is all right not to believe in God; God is just a general principle of good in life. He may have created the world, but He is unrelated to us and does not get involved in human affairs; we are on our own in this world. "For most Americans, God is not to be feared or, for that matter, loved."[37]

This has a direct correlation, of course, with our view of practical ethics. When it comes to making ethical decisions of right and wrong, our supposed belief in God has no influence upon us. Religion plays no role in shaping our opinions on the major social and moral issues of the day. Here is a breakdown of the percentage of people for whom God or religion plays *no* role in shaping their opinion on these social issues: birth control, 58 percent; abortion, 56 percent; homosexuality, 55 percent; pornography, 54 percent; premarital sex, 53 percent; racism, 48 percent; divorce, 43 percent; and "right to die," 43 percent.[38] In other words, we form our ethical or moral views on these various subjects without reference to God, the Bible, or religious faith.

Research shows that most people don't follow what the church says because they aren't aware of its positions on social issues. Only one in five of us ever consults a minister, priest, or rabbi on moral issues. Little more than 10 percent of us believe in all of the Ten Commandments. Forty percent believe in five or less. Why are we so far away from God and the Bible? Because half of us have not been to a religious service in over three months, and a third have not been in over a year.[39]

Any discussion of ethical and social issues requires the use of the word "sin." Therefore, it is important to know the common working definition for this word. Fewer than two in five of us believe sin is "going against God's will" or "going against the Bible" or "violating the Ten Commandments." Most people these days define sin as "breaking your own conscience."[40] This is a natural conclusion if we establish ourselves as *the* authority on morality. If I make up my rules and set my own standards, I can make them anything I want. In this manner, nothing is a sin if I don't want it to be. Research for *Habits of the Heart* yielded the same conclusion. "Liberalized versions of biblical morality tend to subordinate themes of divine authority and human duty to the intrinsic goodness of human nature."[41]

What about our views on heaven and hell? Eighty-two percent of those surveyed say they believe in an afterlife with heaven and hell. Again, this is misleading, because their understanding of what causes a person to go to heaven or hell is not a biblical one. How many of these people believe they are on their way to hell? Four percent! The rest either believe they are going to heaven or are not sure.[42]

Think About It

Looking back over the results of *The Day America Told the Truth,*
1. What surprises you the most?
2. What surprises you the least?
3. What examples can you think of from the lives of your non-Christian friends that verify these conclusions?
    a.
    b.
    c.
4. What dangers do these results indicate may be in the future for our society?
    a.
    b.
    c.

Our Snapshot

So there you have it—a picture of our society and our Christian community in that society through the eyes of both generation X and baby boomers. With their honest responses, is it any wonder that the level of moral absolutes in this country has dropped steadily over the last three decades? Is it any wonder that this generation of Christians are being impacted and influenced so negatively by their culture? *The Day America Told the Truth*, together with the results from the Barna research and our university surveys, clearly portrays similar patterns in baby boomers and generation X. This research shows us why Christians of all generations are wavering with regard to moral principles and ethical certainty.

This chapter has presented our snapshot. In the next chapter we will look at the building blocks upon which these decisions have been based, along with the thinking processes that have allowed us to reach this point in our history.

3

A Penny for Your Thoughts

The Way We Think Becomes the Way We Live

Remote Controls

I have always been fascinated with remote-controlled toys. The operator stands at a distance and directs the movements of the toy. So naturally I introduced our son, Brent, to remote-controlled toys at an early age—a *very* early age. Sue and I were in a toy store prior to his first Christmas, looking for a gift, when I spotted the *perfect* gift—a remote-controlled robot. It was the most fascinating toy in the store. It had red flashing lights on its chest, arms that swung back and forth, and a spherical red head that revolved and flashed a red light. And it emitted a loud, beeping sound as it moved. What a great toy! I immediately employed my best sales tactics on Sue. She wasn't so sure it was a good idea. She had this unfounded motherly fear that this strange-looking toy might frighten her baby. So I turned on my charm and finally convinced her that Brent would *love* it.

We purchased and wrapped the robot for Christmas. The exciting day finally arrived. Brent unwrapped his special gift, and I quickly set it up for a demonstration. He saw me at one side of the kitchen and his mother at the other. Defenseless in the middle of the kitchen floor, he watched as this strange object approached, beeping, flashing, and swinging its arms. It nearly scared him out of his skin! He ran to Sue and all but climbed her to get out of the destructive path of this diabolical figure. Though he was not a great walker yet, he proved to be a pretty good climber that morning. Needless to say, the robot was not Brent's favorite Christmas present that year. In fact, he *never* warmed up to it. We finally had to find it a more loving, accepting home.

Thankfully, however, that toy did later spark Brent's interest in remote-controlled objects. One of the advantages of growing up during the development of remote-control technology has been his purchase of each new advancement. In the last 18 years he has had a variety of objects with remote-controlled units. In fact, just recently I saw him with his remote-controlled car chasing the neighborhood cat down the street!

Popular Influences on People

Remote-controlled objects fascinate us much like sleight-of-hand magic. Our attention is drawn to the robot, plane, car, or boat. The source of the movements is a remote control, often unseen in the distance. So while we have our eyes focused on the toy as it makes its maneuvers, we don't fully understand the true picture until we factor in the influence of the remote control.

The same is true for our ethical lifestyle choices. Most of the time our ethical discussions revolve around a particular conduct: stealing, drinking, premarital sex, and so on. As an ethics teacher, I have noticed that almost the entire discussion time on any ethical topic centers around the pros and cons of the action itself. In reality, however, our discussion should quickly move to the reasoning that motivates the particular lifestyle choice. It is absolutely impossible to understand the choices people all around us make, or even our own choices, until we come to terms with the thinking that influences those choices.

This brings us to popular ways of thinking in our society. Before we look at these, however, we need to discuss a related concept: presuppositions. Presuppositions are the assumptions we bring to our thinking. We cannot prove them; we just believe they are true. Herbert Schlossberg says, "Assumptions are *beliefs*; if they were proven they would not be assumptions. And, they are beliefs so taken for granted that it is not deemed necessary to prove them."[1] Everyone has presuppositions. We must start with some assumptions if we are to think reflectively about anything. The question is—do we realize that we and everyone else have them? Furthermore, it is essential that we know what they are—both in us and in others. It is impossible for us to understand fully any position or reason for action without understanding the presuppositions upon which they are based. Presuppositions or assumptions are powerful, because they have so much influence on the way we process the reality of our world.

In this chapter we're going to examine various patterns of thinking or philosophies around which lifestyle choices are made. Along with each pattern we will consider its presuppositions and examples from life. With this knowledge we can begin to understand what is happening in our society.

I picture these philosophies like the foundation of a house. Sue and I enjoy making improvements on our home, so we have added several rooms across the years. Each time we add to our house, we dig at least three feet into the ground and pour large quantities of concrete with metal reinforcement bars in it to establish a firm foundation upon which to build. If the foundation is not solid, it will not support the construction. The same is true for the processes of thinking we use in making ethical lifestyle choices. If the thought process itself is not solid, our moral decisions may be faulty and collapse under the pressures and stresses of life. Keep this image in mind as you read through these various ways of thinking. See if you can discern a problem with them when they are used as a foundation for making moral choices.

Worldviews

Any one of the following philosophies or a combination of them may join together in our minds to form the building blocks for a worldview—an entire way of seeing our world. We're often not aware of it, but everyone has a worldview. It is the lens through which we see our world. I do not have 20/20 vision, so I wear glasses. When I put on my glasses, they correct my faulty vision, making images sharper, clearer, more defined. So, too, my worldview causes me to interpret in certain ways all the sights, sounds, and information that come into my life. It helps me integrate all of this into a unified picture of reality. I often hear people say, "I don't want any interpretation; just give me the facts." Such a statement is too simplistic. As Schlossberg reminds, "There can be no simple appeal to the 'facts,' for factuality cannot be considered apart from a philosophy by which the facts are interpreted."[2]

A direct link always exists between the way people think and the way they live. Schlossberg reminds us that our practical-minded, antiphilosophical age does not want to hear about philosophy. It's a dirty word. However, it's impossible for us to discuss life without discussing thought. "In the end we live what we believe. . . . Our anti-philosophers are especially vulnerable in this age, because the media fill our environment with popularized philosophies. We do not see our environment . . . because we see *with* it. That means we are influenced by ideas we do not notice and therefore are not aware of their effect on us. Or, if we see the effect, we find it difficult to discover the cause."[3]

The following pages require mental exercise. Exercising our minds is very much like exercising our bodies. Much effort is required, and it may make us sore at first. Nevertheless, the result is worth our effort. Keep that in mind as we now turn to these popular patterns of thinking and worldviews. Trust me— this discussion is absolutely necessary for us to understand what is happening to our society. You may find the reading a bit difficult for a few pages, but it will all come together in later chapters.

Relativism

Presuppositions

- No objective standard of right and wrong exists.
- No position is superior to another. All are without moral definition.
- All beliefs are culturally based and have their origin in human reason.

Explanation

Relativism says we cannot know anything for sure. The jury is still out—on everything. We cannot say that one line of thinking has any more virtue than another or that one line of ethical conduct is better than another. People must decide for themselves what is right or wrong *for them*. What is right for me might be wrong for you. Or what is right for me this morning might be wrong for me tomorrow or even this afternoon. All absolute standards and all judgments are suspended. Everything is relative to the "what" and the "how" of each particular time, place, and person.

This mode of thinking receives support from a variety of sources. One source is the theory of relativity in the scientific field of physics. Albert Einstein proposed that the mass of any body is relative to its movement. Mass varies with movement. Thus, we cannot be certain about an object's mass. It is relative. Another source is the idealist philosophy of Friedrich Hegel. Hegel taught that our world is in constant change. In fact, the only constant in reality is the fact that everything is changing. His famous proposition was "Thesis plus antithesis equals synthesis." Or A plus B are always coming together to create C. Karl Marx used this theory to develop his political system that led to Communism. A third support for relativism comes from the process philosophy of Alfred North Whitehead. Along with Hegel, Whitehead said the essential reality of our world is change. Since God brought the world into existence with images of himself in it, then He too is constantly changing. He awakens to a new world every day just as we do.

When applied to society, this mode of thinking tells us that no cultural rules exist for everyone. Each cultural group polls itself; whatever is voted most acceptable becomes virtue. No one culture is higher than another. All truth is culturally bound. The reason we disagree on various subjects is because we come from different backgrounds. When we expose ourselves to other cultures, we see the error of our exclusive ways and the sin of judging others for holding different values. If a society decides to swap mates, go nude, have multiple mates, or kill their baby girls, they may do so. We are no better than they just because we promote monogamous marriage, clothes, and sanctity of life.

When applied to individuals, this mode of thinking tells us that no set of rules exists for everyone. Each individual decides what is right or wrong for himself or herself. No value system is intrinsically more superior than another, and no one can determine what is right or wrong for another. Our values are conditioned by the circumstances of our lives and by the way we create and process our own reality.

Philosopher Burton Porter offers four reasons for the popularity of this position.

1. *Tolerance.* Our society teaches us to be open-minded to people who are different from us. They have as much right to their beliefs as I do to mine, we are told. What gives me the right to judge them for their differences? Who knows? Maybe they are closer to the truth (if there is such a thing, though probably not) than I am.

2. *A desire to maximize freedom of choice.* If we are going to be truly free human beings, then we cannot be obligated to an objective standard of right and wrong. Rules bind us unnecessarily.

3. *Intellectual uncertainty.* The physical and social sciences are always expanding the pool of knowledge. What was taught as fact yesterday becomes another theory today as new information becomes available. So who is to say we are right about our ideals, values, and judgments?

4. *Awareness of diversity.* The politically correct slogan today is "Celebrate diversity." We must be aware of the multiplicity of lifestyle choices in our world and allow others the same freedom of expression that we desire for ourselves. "It seems presumptuous to state any opinion with deep confidence, and whatever we do maintain is hedged about with a dozen qualifications."[4]

James Bell says relativism implies that it is best that we not have strong convictions about anything, or we will be classified as "a segregationist, bigot, supremacist, and an enemy of the common good."[5] It used to be a virtue in our society to be a person of strong convictions. Not anymore. The popular virtue of our day is to be broad-minded on all viewpoints. We are urged to take them all into our thinking and appreciate them all equally. This perspective is fine when related to cultural expressions like dress, food, holiday traditions, and so on. It becomes another matter entirely when transferred to moral issues. Relativism effectively erases all lines between objective standards of right and wrong.

Example: Patterson and Kim relate the story of a California high school teacher who sent her students home every Friday with this admonition: "Have a great weekend. Be safe. Buckle up. Just say, 'No'—and if you can't say 'No,' then use a condom!" When asked why she gave this advice, she replied, "I try to give support to everyone's value system. So I say, 'If you're a virgin, fine. If you're sexually active, fine. If you're gay, fine.'"[6]

This is the danger of relativism in the realm of ethical lifestyle choices.

Think About It

Think of three examples of people or institutions who exemplify relativism.

1.
2.
3.

Pluralism

Presuppositions

- No objective standard of right and wrong exists.
- Life is full of choices that are all open options to be considered.
- These options are without moral definition.

Explanation

A philosophical extension of relativism is pluralism. Relativism refers to the varied definitions of truth. Pluralism begins with the almost endless list of choices we find in society today. Unlike many other nations of the world where the grocery store or the restaurant or the new car lot offers a very limited number of choices, citizens of the United States are overwhelmed with choices. Take buying a cola drink at the local grocery store. We have a choice of name brands, store brands, or generic brands in original or new-and-improved formula, regular or caffeine-free, sugar-sweetened or diet, bottled in plastic or glass, with either a straight or curved bottle. Then when you check out, you must select either paper or plastic as your sack of choice. What about selecting a television program for the family to watch? Depending on your location, cable company, or satellite service, your choices for any particular hour may range from 10 to 200 programs. Technology prophets say that number will exceed 500 in the near future!

How does pluralism relate to lifestyle choices? As with relativism, pluralism insists that each of these moral choices is of *equal status.* In a hierarchy of values, none is higher. They are all on an even playing field. We are told we should be tolerant and nonjudgmental of each of these choices. Such an attitude not only is politically correct these days but also reflects humility and maturity in our expanding understanding of the peoples and positions of our world. We show our broad-mindedness in thinking this way.

Our exposure to such cultural and religious variety comes from at least two sources. First, advancements in communication and travel have shrunk our world into a global village. The evening news brings us live sights and sounds from around the world via satellite. The Internet gives us access to information almost anywhere in the world. Inexpensive jet travel makes it possible for us to be almost anywhere in the world in a few hours. We can travel to the major cities of the world the way our grandparents visited their state capitals.

A second source for our exposure to cultural and religious variety comes from immigration of large groups of people from around the world. Not only is this true of the United States, but most nations of the world have sizable populations of subcultures. Such groups bring not only their presence but also their language, customs, culture, morals, and religion. In both urban and rural settings in the United States, we see more cultural diversity in one day than many of our grandparents saw in a lifetime.

As it relates to moral lifestyle choices, we are especially affected by religious pluralism. This type of pluralism places all the religions of the world on an equal playing field, with equal validity and an equal access to truth and God/god/gods/no god. As one of my baby boomer students related in class on this matter, "One God; many paths all leading to the same place."

Example: I recently received a scholarly paper written by Bryan Wilson, emeritus fellow at Oxford University. It was sent by the Institute for the Study of American Religion. The accompanying letter stated, "Tolerance amidst diverse expressions of religious beliefs and a multitude of individual religious practices requires an educated eye and an unburdened mind. It challenges us to examine all reflexive notions and definitions of religion and to recognize diversity and even embrace it."

Using the loftiest of language and analysis, the paper attempted to make a case for the equal status of all religious beliefs of the world. Christianity was particularly singled out as being intolerant, exclusivistic, universalistic, and proselytizing.

All such attitudes in church or state around the world must be eradicated, it said. The study of religion must be value-free; none is superior.

The author then proposed a generic definition for religion that had neither God, nor sacred writings, nor rules, nor code of ethical conduct, nor view of humanity or nature of the cosmos, nor eternity. Absolutely anything that enters into the mind of humanity should be equally acceptable as religion and must be embraced. The 42-page paper closed with these words: "In a culturally pluralistic world, religion, like other social phenomena, may take many forms. Just what is a religion cannot be determined by the application of concepts drawn from any one particular tradition."[7] All such concepts must be abandoned, according to religious pluralism.

Think About It

1. What is the first example of pluralism that comes to your mind?
2. Name an example of religious pluralism that you have seen.
3. What is the greatest danger of making all religions equal?

Egoism

Presuppositions

- No objective standard of right and wrong exists.
- God is not actively involved in the world.
- The individual is the primary unit of society.
- An individual's obligation is only to self.
- Individuals can reason and will their way to satisfaction in life.

Explanation

This control unit, egoism, focuses on you as an individual and states that the chief goal of your life is to look out for your own interests. The one person you must seek to please is yourself. In fact, your whole life should be dedicated to promoting your own good. If you do not take care of yourself, who will? Traditionally held views that teach self-denial (giving some of your spending money to the needy) or volunteerism (donating some of your time to a worthy cause) for the sake of helping others are wrong. Such acts are of no value, because they are performed with selfish interests in mind, that is, to make your-self feel good or to look good in the eyes of others.

Ayn Rand, an atheistic humanist, viewed the individual as the center of the universe. Hear her definition of God: "And now I see the face of god, and I raise this god over the earth, this god whom men have sought since men came into being, this god who will grant them joy and peace and pride. This god, this one word: I."[8]

In her book *The Virtue of Selfishness* she said, "The purpose of morality is to define man's proper values and interests, that con-cern with his own interests is the essence of a moral existence, and that man must be the beneficiary of his own moral actions."[9]

Nathaniel Branden wrote an article in the same book titled "Isn't Everyone Selfish?" in which he stated that egoism makes each of us an end unto ourselves. We do what we want to do for our own best interests, as we perceive them to be, and we reap the benefits of those actions. He defines selfishness as acting in your own best interest. This, of course, means that you know what your own best interest is and how to accomplish it with the appropriate values and goals.[10] I am very doubtful that we always know what our own best interests are at every stage of life, at least not enough to serve as an adequate foundation for an entire system of moral theory.

This philosophy is so popular in our society because it is a blank check for self-satisfaction and the pampering of personal desire. It can lead to what Herbert Schlossberg has called "the cult of narcissism or self-expression," which has become so per-vasive. We are told that we ourselves are the measure of both reality and moral principle. "Thus, there are no standards, no belief in eternal truth, no objective measure of right and wrong; norms are delusions, and self-discipline serves no purpose."[11]

Example: Examples of egoism are as close as today's prod-uct advertising. The advertising industry picked up on the self-focus of the "me generation" of the 1970s and 1980s. They learned that egoism sells—everything from toothpaste to motor oil! Listen to these well-known phrases:

"You only go around once; grab all the gusto you can get."
"You deserve a break today."
"Have it your way."
"It's more expensive, but I'm worth it."
"Look out for number one."

"You're the center of your own universe."

"You work hard—you owe it to yourself."

"I'm doing this for me."

And the list goes on endlessly. Notice how all these examples focus attention on pampering or spending money on the most important person in your world—you!

Think About It

What is your favorite egocentric advertising jingle?

Hedonism

Presuppositions

- No objective standard of right and wrong exists.
- No obligation is more important than my own happiness.
- Personal pleasure is the chief goal of life.

Explanation

Closely related to egoism is hedonism, with one important difference. Egoism emphasizes an obligation to self; hedonism goes further in specifying that the chief goal of my life is to seek my own pleasure or happiness.

Burton Porter differentiates four types of hedonism. *Psychological hedonism* says people are so made that they have no choice but to seek pleasure and avoid pain. It is a universal law. *Universalistic hedonism* says the purpose of life is to maximize happiness for society as a whole. *Individualistic hedonism* urges you to seek pleasure for yourself. *Ethical hedonism* says the primary purpose for living should be to search for your own pleasure, which is an intrinsic good.[12] The common thread in all these definitions is that of seeking my pleasure as my highest goal for living.

The Epicureans of ancient Greece popularized this idea with their famous motto, "Eat, drink, and be merry, for tomorrow we die." This was a common philosophy in the apostle Paul's day. He saw it being lived all around him as he traveled on his missionary journeys. He even fought against it in the Corinthian church. See 1 Cor. 15 for evidence of this philosophy. I call it the "party animal" mentality of living for each new physical gratification or each new weekend party. But it goes much deeper. It cuts to the very core of the motivation for living.

Mix this philosophy with free time, a level of income above the necessities of life, an almost endless supply of goods and services, and you have a perfect formula for the materialism of our day. Very quickly our wants become "necessities of life." As the jingle says, "Hush, little luxury—don't you cry. You'll be a necessity by and by."

I wish I could say this philosophy was found only in secular society, but that's not true. Christianity has its own version of hedonism that urges Christians to pamper themselves with the best of everything—God wants His people to go first class. As one popular television evangelist said, "I'm a child of the King, and He wants me to live like a king." This is not a recent development in the Church, however; the "gospel of wealth" has been popular in the United States for over a century. When the social gospel in the late 19th century called for more social responsibility among Christians toward the poor and needy of the country, those preaching a gospel of wealth emphasized the opposite message. Diligence, thrift, honesty, sobriety, and other such virtues lead to prosperity, which is the smile of God on a person's life. Material prosperity may be used to enjoy a comfortable life on this earth while we wait for God's eternal reward. You might say it's a foretaste of heaven now.

Such attitudes toward personal pleasure, with a religious spin, have not furthered the efforts of the gospel of Jesus Christ. Many in our society have been turned off to organized religion, with ample justification. In the survey conducted for *The Day America Told the Truth,* a series of questions was asked related to perceived honesty and integrity in various professions. Television evangelists ranked 71, toward the bottom of a list of 73 professions—below prostitutes and on par with organized crime bosses and drug dealers. And it's not just television evangelists who have slipped in the public eye. Catholic priests ranked 7th, while Protestant ministers came in 19th.[13] This general attitude is verified by the statistic that public confidence in organized religion has dropped 55 percent between 1974 and 1989. We must guard our hearts carefully against surrendering to hedonism, especially in the church.[14]

Example: With this philosophy, we buy into the notion that happiness is a direct result of consuming goods and services for our own pleasure. So we go for all the gusto we can get. This view of personal happiness at the center stage of life fuels multimillion-dollar industries. Money flows into merchants' cash registers like water over Niagara Falls.

So what's the problem with this? Who gets hurt? Many people do. Besides its being an inadequate philosophy for life, it also destroys homes and innocent lives. Recently I was discussing with a friend the reason for her divorce, which at that time was in process. Her reply? "Oh, my husband just doesn't make me happy anymore. He's a good provider, and he takes good care of me and the kids. He loves us dearly. But I'm somehow not happy, so I'm getting out. A person deserves to be happy, don't you think?" This is a common story of our day from the lives of those who place their own personal happiness as the central motivator for living.

If we are not careful, hedonism can propel us to buy objects and seek pleasures that don't satisfy. We get on a roller coaster of spending and doing that takes us up and down with pleasure and dissatisfaction but does not let us get off. It is much like a story related to Daniel Yankelovich by a psychotherapist friend. It seems one of her patients, a woman in her mid-20s, was dissatisfied with her life: "Too many big weekends, too many discos, too many late hours, too much talk, too much wine, too much pot, too much lovemaking." When asked why she didn't just stop all of this, she had a moment of inspired revelation and said, "You mean I really don't have to do what I want to do?"[15]

Too often, if we aren't careful, this philosophy will drive us farther than we ever intended to go. But then, that's what happens when we make our own happiness the driving force of life. Lack of satisfaction then drives us farther in the illusive search for something else that will truly satisfy the longing of our hearts.

Think About It

1. Think of an example of hedonism you have seen with one of your friends.
2. Think of an example of hedonism you have seen at your church.

Determinism

Presuppositions

- No objective standard of right and wrong exists.

- People make choices on the basis of prior conditioning.
- Factors outside us and beyond our control bring this conditioning.
- Humans are creatures of stimulus response just like "other animals."

Explanation

Determinism teaches that everything we do has been pre-programmed into us by prior circumstances. Since we have no choice in the matter, we cannot be held responsible for our actions. This position denies that we have a free will, or at least one that is truly free. Oh, we may think we're calling the shots in our lives, but it's a false assumption. We're actually only performing as we were programmed to. No reason exists to praise an individual for choosing to do the supposed *right* thing or blaming him or her for doing the supposed *wrong* thing. All is without moral value.

Determinism has been taught from a number of different angles. Sigmund Freud, famous psychologist, said we act as we do because of events that happened to us earlier in our lives. We are only acting out now what has been built into us. Noted behaviorist B. F. Skinner said we are nothing more than stimulus-response organisms. Factors come into our lives, and we respond to them, like metal shavings respond to a magnet. Nothing more, nothing less. Karl Marx, one of the engineers of socialism, said universal laws govern the economic structures of the world and make things happen as they do. Philosopher G. W. Leibniz argued that things happen in our world at God's direction, because He is good and this is the best of all possible worlds. Reformer John Calvin taught that God is sovereign over His world, so nothing happens by chance. Because God is in control, the things we see happening must be at His bidding. If not, then He has lost control, which is a theological absurdity.

In its various contexts, determinism sometimes sounds like a logical component of thought. However, carried to its logical extreme, it is one of the foundations for the victim mentality so prevalent in our society today. If these deterministic factors control my life, I cannot be held responsible for my behavior. Someone or something else is to blame for my situation or my actions.

Example: I was calling a friend's attention to an inappropriate behavior when she stopped me in midsentence. "You can't blame me for what I do. I grew up in a dysfunctional family. I didn't receive the proper parental nurturing as a child. Therefore I'm not responsible for my actions." Whether she understood the philosophical underpinnings of her statement is doubtful. However, she certainly had mastered the language of determinism.

For years we have believed that the illness of alcoholism starts with a personal choice to drink alcoholic beverages on a regular basis. Now we are being told by some medical personnel that alcoholics were never in a position to help themselves—they were predetermined by their genes to drink, or by a chemical imbalance or some other condition that made them victim to an illness beyond their willful control.

That same argument has been extended to teen and adult drug users. A hospital in our area has been running a radio advertisement that promotes this view. It urges parents of teen drug users not to blame their children—they can't help themselves; they have an illness like cancer or diabetes. They were driven to illegal drugs by a physical need that can be treated at this particular hospital.

This argument is even being extended to adulterers. National attention is being given to the theory that many individuals who cheat on their mates cannot help themselves. They are victims of a genetic flaw; therefore they cannot be held responsible for their wayward lifestyles. If determinism is a correct view of reality, then things truly are out of our control. We are all victims in one way or another. We can blame someone or something for all our shortcomings or failures.

Think About It

1. Do you know anyone who believes in determinism?
2. If so, why do you suppose he or she holds to this view?
3. In your opinion, what is the greatest advantage to believing in determinism?
4. In your opinion, what is the greatest error in believing in determinism?

Secular Humanism

Presuppositions

- No objective standard of right and wrong exists.

- God either does not exist or is out of the picture.
- Each person creates his or her own reality.
- The natural world of space and time is all there is to reality.

Explanation

This philosophy places humanity at the center of the universe more completely than any other system of thought. Humanity is answerable only to itself. If God exists—and He more than likely does not, according to this view—He is an absentee landlord from creation. We are on our own to do as we please. The future is open to us. We have the power to reach our potential in science and technology and determine our own destiny. This view limits reality to what we can experience and demonstrate through our senses. If we cannot see, taste, or touch it, it is not meaningful.

Secular humanism is not completely unique from the other philosophies already discussed. Rather, it blends several of the components of other systems of thought into a new one. That is the reason you will see several familiar features.

In many ways, secular humanism actually elevates humanity to divinity. Herbert Schlossberg says that people do not usually blatantly claim that we are deity. Instead, they give us divine characteristics like "sovereignty (or autonomy), complete rationality, and moral perfection." Nineteenth-century French philosopher Auguste Comte went to the extreme in deifying the human race. He proposed "the Religion of Humanity," in which he urged people to worship the humanity of the past, present, and future.[16]

A humanist ethic is self-created. Thus, all universal norms are denied. I must decide what is right and wrong for me. This decision is almost always a practical one, based on what works in my life. The common characteristic of the various humanist ethics is their appeal to subjectivism. No form of objective law can possibly be accepted. This effectively makes each person a law unto himself or herself. As Schlossberg summarizes it, "If I succumb to the humanist delusion, the ultimate egoism of believing that my own sentiments have the force of supreme law—that is, if I succumb to the serpent's temptation by declaring myself a god who determines good and evil—I can do anything at all with confidence in its legitimacy. The supreme lawgiver—I, myself—has ruled."[17]

Example: The clearest presentation of humanist ideology in recent years appeared in 1973 as the *Humanist Manifesto II*, written by Paul Kurtz and Edwin Wilson and signed by hundreds of the leading intellectuals of the day. The manifesto was more concerned with denying God and condemning religion with its traditional moral values than with affirming anything. Rather than denying that deity exists, it simply replaced the Judeo-Christian view of God with humanity as god. An example of this: "Humans are responsible for what we are or will become. No deity will save us; we must save ourselves."[18] With lofty language, the manifesto taught the perfectibility of humanity through the use of reason, science, and technology. Ethics became nothing more than doing whatever an individual or consenting adults want to do. As they put it, "A civilized society should be a *tolerant* one."[19]

If the damaging atheistic positions of the *Humanist Manifesto II* remained in intellectual circles, they would probably do little damage. However, they have not remained there. They have found their way into the mainstreams of our politics, economics, popular culture, and even religions. The views presented in the manifesto are advocated almost every night on prime-time television. They are subtle but nonetheless real. We must constantly be on our guard against the influence of humanism in our society and in our personal lives.

Think About It

List three places where you see secular humanism in society today, and state how each might pose a danger.
1.
2.
3.

Nihilism

Presuppositions

- No objective standard of right and wrong exists.
- Life is without purpose or meaning.
- All choices and actions in life are meaningless.

Explanation

Nihilism is a philosophy like no other. All the others find

meaning or value in something in life, even if it is a misdirected meaning or value. Friedrich Nietzsche characterized nihilism as a position in which "everything is permitted." Every act in life is of the same value: meaningless. Saving a life equals blowing your nose equals getting a college education equals giving money to charity equals watching television all day. It doesn't matter what you do—it is all of no value. This philosophy is the "absolutization of nothingness."

I read about this philosophy as a college student but had no point of reference for seeing it in my world. My professors described its manifestations in life, but I saw no current examples. That has all changed. Now many rock musicians are espousing this philosophy. They argue that without value or meaning in life, we might as well perform any act that comes into our minds. Let your imagination be your guide. If something enters your head, just do it; there's no good reason not to do it.

Of course, this idea devalues not only meaning in life but also life itself. It destroys the individual and everything in its wake. It fuels self-destruction. That is why this way of thinking so often leads to murder and suicide. Some rock stars even promote murder and suicide in their music as the ultimate manifestation of their view of reality.

Example: Nihilism is often operative in gangs in the United States. Gang violence ravages our streets in large metropolitan cities as well as in small rural villages. Recently a violent act in Los Angeles outraged the entire city, including gang members who did not participate in this crime. In this particular event, a family of five was returning home from a barbecue late at night. They accidentally made a wrong turn near their home and headed down a gang-controlled street. The gang called this street "the avenue of the assassins." Gang members threw trash cans in front of the car to stop it. Then they completely surrounded the car. With guns in hand, they opened fire from every direction, sending a shower of bullets through every window in the car. All the family members were injured; a three-year-old girl was killed. Senseless death? Yes, but what difference does it make? Human life has no meaning and is of no value. The heroic acts of the paramedics who rushed to the crime scene were of no greater value than the acts of violence themselves.

Even this example of gang violence does not fully capture the essence of nihilism. Gang members later disclosed that the reason they attacked this family was because the family had been disrespectful—they had entered gang territory without permission. So in their twisted way of thinking, the gang did value or find meaning in their territory. They also found meaning in their group identity. A true nihilist finds meaning in absolutely nothing in life. Think about it—it's a dead-end street as a philosophy for life. But as our society degenerates in its thinking, more and more people are adopting it for use in their lives.

Think About It

1. Why do you suppose nihilism is called a dead-end philosophy?
2. Where does this philosophy logically lead a person?
3. Do you know anyone who thinks in this way?
4. If so, can you think of any way to help them?

All Except One

This completes our philosophical discussion. These are not the only ways people are influenced in making ethical decisions. Several others exist;[20] however, these are the most popular ones in our society today. The most obvious omission from this list is the Christian view, which focuses on God, the Bible, and objective standards of right and wrong. Chapters 5 and 6 will be devoted to this presentation. The reason the Christian view has been purposefully omitted from this chapter is because it's not a system of thought our current popular culture uses widely in its thinking or ethical decision-making today. In fact, a significant number of leaders and spokespersons for society are doing everything in their power to erase all references to God and biblical principles from our national consciousness. The Christian view offers a much-needed alternative to the views presented.

It is now time to turn our attention to culture itself and see how these philosophies find their way into life.

4

On Guard

Preparing for the Culture Battle

Price Tags

One of my favorite television commercials these days is that of a fast-food hamburger restaurant. To illustrate the point that all their hamburgers are selling for 99 cents, it shows two six-year-old boys holding their own garage sale, obviously without their parents' knowledge or permission. They've spread all their toys across the front yard and taped 99-cent sale tags on everything, including a baby sister! Some of their toys are worth less than 99 cents and some much more. No matter. Everything is going for one low price, including the sister.

The ad is amusing because we realize that not everything in our world has the same value or the same price tag. A value is the relative worth we place on experiences, people, relationships, and possessions. It is what causes us to see some things as more important in life than others.

Let me illustrate. Remember as a teenager when you just *had* to have a particular type of shirt or dress because everyone else had it? You thought you'd die if you didn't get it! Or at least that's what you told your parents. The article of clothing, or your friends seeing you wearing it, was of great value to you. Then, some time later, it ended up in a rag box or donation sack; its value had dropped to the bottom of your scale.

Value Systems and Lifestyle Choices

The philosophies and our worldview that we discussed in the last chapter play a major role in setting the values or price tags we place on things in life. If you know what philosophy a person has adopted, you can accurately predict where his or her values lie. Once you understand a person's value system, you can understand his or her lifestyle choices. Note the following observations about values.

1. *A value is not really yours unless you choose to accept it for yourself.* Your parents, pastor, or good friend may have a value and may want you to have it as well, but you alone decide whether it is a personal value or not. Most people misunderstand the rebellious stage many adolescents experience. They sometimes exhibit strange behavior. It is not that they want to do the opposite of what their parents want them to do. Rather, it is part of a process for children to try values for themselves and make them their own.

I've watched numerous times as teenagers "go off the deep end," so to speak, for a period of trial and error with values. One particular example of this occurs with a few of our students every fall on our university campus. Parents bring their children to the university from all over our region of the nation. Their cars are filled with clothes, personal supplies, dorm room furnishings, hopes, and dreams. Everything is placed in the dorm room. Tears are shed. Good-byes are said. The parents head back home. Some students watch as their parents head out the circle drive, then have an amazing realization. All of a sudden it occurs to them that parental observation, even parental control, is over. They immediately respond by doing everything they ever wanted to do that their parents would not allow. In a week or two parents get word that their child is living out of bounds. Some parents, not realizing what is happening, blame the college for a permissive environment. They brought us a well-mannered, perfectly adjusted student, and the university environment corrupted their child in two short weeks!

What really happened? Students who respond in this manner have been living their parents' value system while at home. They performed as expected to win parental approval. But given the freedom, without parental control, they opted for a different value system. The university environment did not corrupt their actions—the true desires of their hearts did it. They had never truly adopted their parents' values as their own.

Some students find the adoptive process harder than others. But regardless of the difficulty of this stage, more often than not these students come full circle and accept a personal value system very similar to their parents'. There is a difference, however: now the system is their own.

2. *Parental values must be transferred to children.* Parents would like to save their children a lot of heartache and just *give* them *their* value system. That's exactly what they do with their children when they are young. They set the rules for almost all personal behavior. When children question the *why* of a particular directive, parents often respond with "Because I told you so." What kind of an answer is that? It's an answer that indicates the children are living by their parents' values. Making choices in this fashion works fine for small children, but it doesn't work very well for teenagers; it doesn't work at all for adults. A time should occur in all our lives when we launch out to live by our own set of freely chosen values.

I used the phrase "should occur" in the previous sentence to indicate that it doesn't happen in everyone's life. Some people unfortunately live their entire lives making choices according to the values of others. They may make choices according to what their parents, pastor, or friends tell them they should do. But they don't think for themselves, and they don't live by their own value system.

I remember one particularly painful experience of one of my baby boomer students related to this topic. I had given an assignment for students to come to class with a list of their most important values and the source from which each came. While working on the assignment, this lady in her mid-40s came to the realization that none of her values were her own; they were all her mother's. In other words, she governed her actions based on what her mother told her to do rather than on what she believed was right; she lived to please her mother. This realization was traumatic for my student. She didn't know what she believed or why. She began that day to develop her own value system.

3. *Values are chosen from among alternatives.* Simply put, if you go shopping at the mall with a $20 bill burning a hole in your pocket, you cannot buy two CDs, a watch, a book, a flower arrangement, and an afternoon snack. You have to buy the one or two most important items on your list and let the others wait. The same is true with values. Everything in life cannot be at the top of our value list. From childhood throughout adulthood, we see many alternative forms of behavior, relationships, and pos-

sessions and decide which ones will become most important to us.

4. *Value researchers indicate that during value establishment, we go through various stages of development.* First, we accept the values imposed on us by our parents. We do something because parents make us do it or at least *strongly* recommend it! Next, we reach a stage in which we prefer these values for ourselves. We choose to eat beets even when Mom doesn't put them on our plate. Last, the highest stage is when we commit ourselves to a value. Now it is our own personal conviction. I'm freely committed to this course of action by my own choice.

Stages of Value Development

1. *Imposed*

2. *Personal Preference*

3. *Personal Commitment*

Let me illustrate the above principle with an example from our son Brent's life. Sue and I decided he should learn to swim when he was three years old. He hated the swimming pool, and he hated the idea of swim lessons. In fact, he cried every day on the way to the lessons as he begged us not to make him learn to swim. We made him go anyway. He caught on quickly, and before we knew it, he was swimming across the deep end of the pool. By the time he was eight years old, he was asking us to take him and his friends to the city pool for the afternoon. Today he goes swimming every chance he gets, and we take family vacations every year to the ocean. This past summer he decided to get his license and work as a lifeguard at the local YMCA pool.

The point? We imposed the value on Brent at first, then he made it his preference, and finally he embraced it as a personal conviction.

Think About It

1. List five things that you highly value (people, relationships, possessions, and so on).

   a.

   b.

   c.

    d.

    e.

2. Has your experience of making values your own been easy or difficult? Why?
3. Think of an illustration from your own life in which one of your values was first imposed, then you made it a preference, and finally it became a personal commitment.

Sources of Values

We must consider the sources from which we derive our values as we think about our personal value system. Though we are often not aware of them, many definite reasons exist for the choices we make in life. We usually take our value system for granted and make choices unconsciously, so it's a good idea to consider the methods we use for making our choices.

A. A higher authority. A higher authority is an obvious source of values for Christians, who seek to live their lives according to the will of God. But we cannot simply say we look to God for our system of values. Within this major heading are several types of authority bases, for we recognize that God directs in various ways.

We often find God's will through reading *the Bible.* Thus, we appeal to the authority of Scripture for our moral choices. We believe that in His Word God has given humanity a blueprint for living. As we read and apply it to our lives, we find the direction we need for making moral choices in our complex world. This form of Christian authority should be our first and most important source for a personal value system.

A second Christian authority is *the tradition of the Christian community.* Christian tradition is the "beliefs, values, and customs transmitted from one generation to the next."[1] It is very important to the Church, since it provides a stabilizing influence for the faith to be passed to the next generation. Creeds, interpretation of Scripture, theological formulations, symbols, rituals, and the like all represent components of Christian tradition. The ministry of the Holy Spirit is essential in guarding God's truth as it is passed down through the ages.

A third Christian authority is *the individual direction of the Lord.* This can be a tricky one! This is the authority in which you feel the Lord impressing a particular course of action on your mind. It sounds good to say, "The Lord is directing me to do this." The problem arises when such supposed directions are not in keeping with Scripture or the character of God. Unfortunately, some people use this authority to justify their own selfish desires and then seek to lay the blame for misconduct on the Lord. So we must be careful to test this source with the Bible and common sense.

B. Logic or reason. Another source for moral choice is the brain God gave us with which to think for ourselves. We have the ability to look at the facts, predict probable conclusions, and make choices on the basis of what appears to be the reasonable thing to do.

The greatest danger here is in allowing our logical or reasoning ability to be clouded by preconceived desired outcomes. In other words, we work backward from a course of action we desire to a reasonable plan to justify it. Given enough time, the human heart has an amazing ability to justify almost anything it desires. Thus, while reason is an essential source for making value choices, it must always be balanced with the authority of Scripture and the tradition of the Christian community.

C. Personal experience. Sometimes our values are derived from trial and error. Hopefully, we learn from our successes and failures in life. If we do, we become wiser with time. Otherwise, we are doomed to repeat our same failures over and over again. This source of values is often referred to as "the hard knocks of life." Thankfully, when it comes to making moral choices, we don't have to learn everything the hard way. We can listen to God's Word and other Christians and avoid the heartache of experiencing failure firsthand. The value of avoiding premarital sex, adultery, illegal drugs, and a host of other sins should never have to be learned through experience.

D. Emotion. Emotion is an interesting source for values. In this scheme of thinking, people make choices according to what they want to do or the way they feel. It's a fairly easy and uncomplicated way of life: just do whatever you want to do, whenever you want to do it. When asked to justify your choices, simply say, "I did it because I felt like it." This is called an "emotive" ethic, because it is based on personal emotions. Believe it or not, a great number of people live their lives in this manner.

E. Sense perception. Values are chosen in this method by using the senses. We choose on the basis of evidence gathered by seeing, hearing, touching, tasting, or smelling. God has given us wonderful instruments to use to make wise choices. However, they cannot always give us enough information to make wise moral choices. We must be careful with this source when it comes to ethical matters. We can do what I call selective sensing. That is, we pay attention to what we prefer in order to influence the outcome in a certain direction.

F. Peers. As a source of values, peers are very similar to the first source. We turn to someone else for guidance in making choices. Here, though, the source is other people instead of God. Often it is a lower instead of a higher authority; other humans do not always offer good directions for life.

We have known since childhood the vital importance of our friends' opinions. No matter how far-out the hair or fashion style became, if our friends had it, we wanted it too. This is an easy source of values, because you don't have to think for yourself—you just follow the crowd and go with the flow. To some degree, most of us are influenced by peer pressure throughout life. We don't want to be totally unique in our lifestyle. However, by the time we reach adulthood, we should be making our own value judgments.

G. Significant others. Values also come our way from parents, grandparents, other family members, teachers, coaches, and other significant people in our lives. God places older people along our path to give us wise counsel in setting our standards for life. Remember when you were a child and it seemed adults controlled your every move? At home your parents, guardians, or grandparents told you what to do. At school your teachers told you what to do. At church your Sunday School teacher or pastor told you what to do. Sometimes you resented it, and sometimes you realized it was for your own good. Somewhere along the way they quit imposing their values, and you adopted your own value system for proper conduct. Looking back, we realize the important contribution these significant others have made in our lives.

H. The media. The media comes at us from almost every direction. Its message comes through television, radio, compact discs, newspapers, magazines, billboards, movies, and the computer. It offers value suggestions and persuasive arguments on what to eat, how to dress, how to comb our hair, how to treat our family members, how to spend our money and time, and just about every other choice we make in life. We can avoid media's influence only by moving deep into the woods or out into the desert. Media has more contact hours each day with the average child in this country than parents, church, or schoolteachers. It is a powerful shaper of our value system.

Think About It

1. Look back over the eight sources of values discussed above. Which two are most influential in the average teenager's life?

    a.

    b.

2. Which two were most influential in establishing your own personal values?

    a.

    b.

Note: When I ask the first question in class, my baby boomer students with teenagers in the home always give the same answer: media and peers. This is evidenced in the information below from the most recent research. Notice the change in the most influential sources over the years. Also, notice how quickly media moved to first place and how church dropped out of the picture.

TOP SOURCES FOR PERSONAL VALUES			
YEAR	FIRST PLACE	SECOND PLACE	THIRD PLACE	FOURTH PLACE
1960	Family	School	Friends/Peers	Church
1980	Friends/Peers	Family	Media	School
1990	Media	Friends/Peers	Family	School[2]

Putting It All Together

The philosophies presented in the last chapter influence our thinking and living. They assist us in placing price tags on everything in our own personal world. The crucial question then becomes "How do we come in contact with these philosophies?" Few of us took a philosophy class in high school to learn to think in these ways. Yet every high schooler I have ever known has been adept in applying one or more of these philosophies to life. So when did it happen? Junior high? Elementary school? Daycare center? Were we born with these ways of processing reality hardwired into our brain?

I would argue that these ways of thinking are not hard-wired into us, though they do appeal to natural tendencies in our human nature. For example, it does not require a philosophy class to teach a three-year-old to apply egoism to life. The tendency to self-preference is already present. If you don't believe me, volunteer to work in a nursery with two- and three-year-olds at your church. I did. What an education! Their most frequently used words are "I," "me," "my," and "mine." Their whole world revolves around their own personal wants and needs.

When, then, do we become so philosophically sophisticated in our thinking? Maybe we're asking the wrong question. Maybe it isn't *"When* does it happen?" but *"Where* does it happen?"

I think you already know the answer to the "where" question. It happens in the environment of our culture. Culture is the soil in which we are all planted the day we begin life on this earth. It is as much a part of our lives as the air we breathe. Christopher Dawson, a noted intellectual historian, says, "A social culture is an organized way of life which is based on a common tradition and conditioned by a common environment. . . . It is clear that a common way of life involves a common view of life, common standards of behavior and common standards of value."[3] We receive cultural values from every sight, sound, and smell that comes to us from the earliest age. These cultural values become the standards by which we place our price tags on everything in our world. Kenneth Myers asks,

> What sort of being is a culture? It's not a person. It's not even an institution, like the church or the state or the family. It is instead a dynamic pattern, an ever-changing matrix of objects, artifacts, sounds, institutions, philosophies, fashions, enthusiasms, myths, prejudices, relationships, attitudes, tastes, rituals, habits, colors, and loves, all embodied in individual people, in groups and collectives and associations of people (many of whom do not know they are associated), in books, in buildings, in the use of time and space, in wars, in jokes, and in food.[4]

Allan Bloom says culture should be the highest expression of human creativity. He says culture is used in two ways: first, as a people or nation (such as the French or German culture); and second, as art, music, educational television, and everything uplifting or edifying, as opposed to commerce. He argues that good culture, culture as it is intended to be, should also be a synthesis of reason and religion.[5] Much of our popular culture today is an absence of both.

Culture is the design of neither Satan nor humanity. God himself designed culture for the good intentions of humanity. He placed Adam and Eve together in a social bond and gave them the directive to re-create. In the Garden of Eden culture and worship of God went hand in hand. They were two sides of human expression. All that humanity did was in loving obedience to God.[6] Only after the Fall did culture become separate from worship and a tool in the hands of Satan to keep humanity from true relationship with God.

Putting Culture on the Hot Seat

Is culture, then, to blame for all the sin and problems of society today? No. Culture, in and of itself, is value-neutral. It is the particular positions that a culture takes that create a problem. For example, culture itself may tell us we need to wear clothes when in public, but not what kind of clothes to wear. The particular expression of that admonition comes from the culture influencing you. An Asian culture might dictate a kimono; a rural American culture might call for flannel and blue jeans; an urban culture might require a dress suit; a motorcycle club might suggest a leather outfit.

Who sets the standards for a particular culture? That's a hard question to answer. Nobody and everybody. When we study culture in its total context, we are impressed that it is the result of billions of choices, separate choices by millions of people. Rarely is the condition of a particular culture the product of deliberate decision, either by society itself or by individuals such as social engineers wearing white lab coats and thick glasses. Cultural development flows naturally, not artificially.[7] William Bennett, former United States secretary of education, comments, "Our common culture is not something manufactured by the upper stratum of society in the elegant salons of Washington, New York, or Cambridge. Rather it embodies truths that most Americans can recognize and examine for themselves. These truths are passed down from generation to generation, transmitted in the family, in the classroom, and in our churches and synagogues."[8] I might add that popular culture today is taking fewer cues from tradition, family, and church, and more cues from media and peers. So the answer to our question of who sets cultural standards is nobody in particular, but everybody in general by the decisions we make on a daily basis.

Information is always coming to us from different cultural influences. We hear from the culture of our nationality, the popular culture of the media, the Christian culture of our church, and a host of others. They all offer suggestions on what to eat, how to dress, how to fix our hair, how to speak, how to be entertained, and every other choice we make in life. But more important, they suggest how we should *think*. As Kenneth Myers puts it, "Popular culture's greatest influence is in the way it shapes *how* we think and feel (more than *what* we think and feel) and how we think and feel about thinking and feeling."[9] And it all happens so unconsciously.

Cultural Battles

Vying for control of whole societies of people has led to the phenomenon of cultural battles. Their purpose centers on who and what influences the standards of a particular culture. As William Bennett sees it, this battle involves the struggle over "the principles, sentiments, ideas, and political attitudes that define the permissible and the impermissible, the acceptable and the unacceptable, the preferred and the disdained, in speech, expression, attitude, conduct, and politics."[10]

Why is there a cultural battle in our society today? Because of the different beliefs that exist between various groups and between the rich or the powerful or the influential who dominate many institutions and exert influence on life and culture. The battle rages in the academic, intellectual, and literary worlds; in Hollywood; in the artistic community; in the educational system; in the political system; in every arena where culture has an influence.[11]

We're not just spectators in this battle over culture—we're players as well. That's because we're not simply on the receiving end of culture. We're also on the sponsoring end, which in a way makes each one of us producers of culture. Let me explain. If you visit your local grocery store and go down the cereal aisle, you will see some pretty wild excuses for morning nutrition. Some of it should be moved to the candy aisle; some of it should be taken to the dog food aisle; some of it should be immediately thrown into the dumpster behind the store! So why is that junk on the shelf? Because *we* want it there. That's right. Every time someone buys a box of Go-Go Goobers, he or she is casting a vote to keep that particular product on the market. If enough people eat it, then it makes a profit for the producer. And producers are more than happy to keep cranking out anything we'll buy. When a critical finger is pointed at those responsible for bad breakfast cereal, it has to be pointed at the producer *and* at us consumers.

Now take that same line of logic and apply it to bad programming in television, for example. If people didn't watch it, advertisers wouldn't have an audience to whom to sell their products, so they wouldn't sponsor it. Bad programs would be off the air in two weeks. Censorship in the form of restricting the supply is not the definitive answer to bad programming, although some restrictions are necessary. Restricted appetite in the form of low public demand is a more workable solution. So viewers are as much to blame as the producers for bad television. They'll give us whatever we want to see. Thus, we set the standards of our culture by our daily choices. Currently a national debate is occurring over bad television programming. A producer of one of the worst shows responded on a recent newscast, "Check our ratings. We're simply supplying what people want to watch."

This leads to another important point in the culture battle: critical mass. "Critical mass" here refers to the number of people needed to make an influence on the culture. If you've ever played a game of tug-of-war over a mudhole, you know what I mean. Each team is evenly balanced in terms of weight and strength. But add one more football player to our side, and we win. In like manner, sponsors of a cultural position are always looking for one more person for their side. If they can get you and your friends to dress as they want you to dress, or talk as they want you to talk, or act as they want you to act, they have strengthened their case and enlarged their influence. When enough people join their side, they can establish their position as a cultural norm for society.

This phenomenon is much like a snowball rolling down a mountainside, building strength as it goes. As sponsors of cultural positions add supporters to their position, they add strength to their argument by showing us that *everyone* believes this way or does this thing. More than likely, *not* everyone is on their side. But in time the argument can be used to get *almost* everyone on it. It is a powerful tool for promoting a particular position in the culture war.

Think About It

1. What do you see as the three most powerful influencers of culture?

   a.

   b.

   c.

2. What three cultural mediums have the most influence in your life?

   a.

   b.

   c.

3. Think of a television program that has a negative moral influence but stays on the air because it's popular.

   a. What values does it teach?

   b. What influence is it having on our society?

What Is at Stake

Many social analysts see the culture battles as turf protection for certain classes, races, genders, or ways of life. Some see it as an economic battle to sell CDs, clothes, or cars. That's true, but it's more—much more. As Kenneth Myers puts it,

> Culture has very much to do with the human spirit. What we find beautiful or entertaining or moving is rooted in our *spiritual* life. Most modern social critics are concerned about culture in general and popular culture in particular because of the political and economic consequences of certain cultural arrangements. They are obsessed with questions of power. But there is a realm of human experience that is prior to power. It is the imagination, and it has profound significance in shaping human history and in assisting (or opposing) moral and spiritual ends.[12]

Myers goes on to quote T. S. Eliot in "Notes Towards the Definition of Culture." Eliot proposes that religion and culture are two aspects of the same thing. They appeal to the same desires and needs in humanity.[13]

Culture has existed since the Garden of Eden. So why the current discussion? Because popular culture in the last three decades has become a powerful force in changing society, more powerful than at any other time in our national history. Myers sees the root of the problem a century earlier with the factory workers of the industrial revolution. The farm offered plenty of work and adequate variety in life. But once displaced in the big city, workers became bored with monotonous factory jobs. They looked for diversions and entertainments in their free time. That was just the beginning of a long development that has brought us to where we are today. "If one is relying on popular culture to stimulate excitement, one will gradually require greater and greater levels of stimulation to achieve the same level of excitement. The makers of popular culture will gladly oblige."[14]

Isn't entertainment simply a harmless diversion? What does it have to do with impacting the human spirit? Everything. You see, popular culture is not satisfied just to entertain us. It becomes power hungry to get inside us and influence us or, worse yet, control our thinking. And in exchange for all it does for us, we worship it, or at least incorporate it into our worship of God. As T. S. Eliot said, religion and culture are two aspects of the same thing.

You're Mine, All Mine

I remember as a child watching cartoons that featured diabolical figures who controlled people by planting a device in their ears through which they gave commands. These people then mindlessly obeyed the commands. Then the technology developed so that these fiends of power could plant the device directly in victims' brains. When the job of planting the device was completed, the villain of the show would laugh and say with a shiver, "Now you're mine—all mine!"

I know it sounds a little far-fetched, but something like that has actually happened to us with popular culture. I said earlier that we vote for the offerings of culture with our daily choices. But that's not the whole picture. After we make a conscious decision in a certain direction, we begin to relinquish self-control and are slowly but surely controlled by that thing to which we give ourselves. A common example regarding our physical bodies is the choice to smoke cigarettes or take illegal drugs. At first it's a conscious decision. However, as addiction sets in, we no longer have control over the practice. It becomes not just a habit—our bodies depend upon it. We go through withdrawal if we try to quit. The cigarettes or drugs control us.

In that same way, we can easily become addicted to our music or television shows. You say, "So? That doesn't affect me physically like cigarettes or drugs." No indeed. These offerings of popular culture have *a far more powerful control* than just physical addiction. They get into our minds and affect the way we think, the way we act, the way we react, and the price tags we place on the people and experiences of life. At a deeper level, they affect the very foundational principles of life—who we are at the core of our existence.

Everyone who studies society today comes to the same conclusion: we are addicted to our entertainment. Take music, for instance. Our society must have it in large doses every day. The average teenager listens to 10,500 hours of music from the 7th to the 12th grade, almost as much time as spent in public school from kindergarten through high school.[15] Some teenagers report that they would rather have their music than eat.[16] It is as important to them as the air they breathe. A large portion of young people's lives is music; it is their passion. Nothing excites them as music does. Adults are addicted too. We have radios, CD players, and cassette players in our living rooms, kitchens, bedrooms, garages, cars, offices, or wherever we go. Most of us listen to music throughout the day.

Look at our addiction to television. The average household in America has the television on 49 hours a week. Households with children have it on nearly 59 hours a week. The average preschool child in the United States watches 6,000 hours of television before starting to school. The average teenager watches 22 hours per week. The average adult watches between 27 and 42 hours per week, depending on age and gender.[17]

Put music and television together, and you have MTV. On August 1, 1981, at 12:01 A.M. the course of the entertainment industry changed when MTV went on the air. It gave us the ability to "watch" music.[18] Media analysts were not sure if it would find a market, but it did—a big market. The music video industry is one of the most powerful influences of popular culture.

I have known about media addiction through my experiences with college students for many years, but I never heard it articulated until this summer while on vacation. We had just arrived at our cottage, and I was channel surfing on the television. I reached MTV just in time to hear the VJ (video jockey) make a fairly broad claim. He said of MTV, "We own this generation." He was not entirely correct, but he had a point. At first we're intrigued by the sights and sounds of a music video. Then we're mesmerized, like a charmed snake. Ultimately we're hooked. Once we surrender to its power, the entertainment industry can control our minds.

Research shows that the average MTV viewer consumes five hours a day. That's a lot of music videos! They're not just strange sights and sounds, either. More important, they contain programmed philosophy. It is a very sophisticated and cleverly packaged conduit of the philosophies we discussed in the last chapter.

You may be thinking, "I don't watch music videos; that doesn't apply to me." Maybe not, but probably some of your friends do, and its influence spills over into your world. I spoke at a district church teen retreat last winter on the subject of the impact of the entertainment industry on our lives. To get a reading of my audience in the first session, I asked how many of them watched MTV regularly. I expected a few hands to go up here and there. I was shocked when three-fourths of the crowd raised their hands. Many people in our church watch it. For those who don't watch, dozens of other cultural mediums just as powerful as MTV make their influence felt in our lives.

Flag on the Play

People are beginning to wake up in record numbers and recognize the cultural problem. Like referees in a game of football, they're beginning to blow their whistles and throw down their yellow flags. Not only do they realize that culture is affecting the ways we act and think, but also they recognize our inability to pull away from the powerful influence of this pervasive force. They see that it is killing us softly. It has reached a level at which we now see that not only are people in our society going over the boundaries of what is morally right, but they no longer know where the boundaries are or even that boundaries exist. The influence of culture has precipitated a major shift in the value system of this generation, a shift that is morally bankrupt. Rowland Nethaway writes, "Adults have always complained about their youth, but this is different. There have always been wild and rebellious kids who would go off the track and do something wrong. But they knew where the track was and what was wrong. Many of today's youth do not seem to know right from wrong. Children robbing, maiming and killing on whims, and no pity and no remorse."[19]

Josh McDowell comments, "One of the prime reasons this generation is setting new records for dishonesty, disrespect, sexual promiscuity, violence, suicide, and other pathologies, is because they have lost their moral underpinnings; their foundational belief in morality and truth has been eroded."[20] How did this happen?

A Silent Revolution

Society in the United States has gone through a silent cultural revolution since the 1960s. This revolution has radically altered the formation and operation of personal value systems. Because baby boomers grew up in this period, they're not aware of the startling changes that have occurred in society. The changes happened too slowly to be noticed.

Space does not permit a full treatment of this subject. A brief overview, however, will explain the problem. Community life in most places in the United States prior to 1960 was governed by a fairly uniform standard of personal conduct. Values and personal choices for most people were based on the Judeo-Christian tradition, whether they professed to be religious or not. Community standards permitted some practices and forbade others. This standard was so uniform that some referred to it as a new civil religion known as "Americanism." George Gallup and Jim Castelli say that this period had "a shared public faith in the nation, a faith linked to people's everyday life through a set of beliefs, symbolized rituals that contained religious elements and overtones but were not formally associated with any particular religion."[21]

The 1960s brought the sexual revolution, situation ethics, the counterculture movement, and a host of other influences that called the Judeo-Christian tradition into question. Such cultural change has been in evolution long enough to give us a fairly pluralistic society. This means that most conduct condemned as immoral 30 years ago is now tolerated as "alternate lifestyles." The general public no longer frowns on unmarried couples living together, unwed motherhood, or the practice of homosexuality.

What does this history lesson have to do with *your* personal value system? Everything. It means you can no longer depend on society or culture for an approved set of mores. Society approves almost anything these days. One of the dangers of our pluralistic society is that such a variety of voices has a detrimental effect on authority. Thus, parents have a more difficult time exercising authority over their children, and the church is not viewed as having much authority either. People want to go their own way and do their own thing.

All this is verified in the survey results of *The Day America Told the Truth*. Our entire culture has lost sight of its moral boundaries. Patterson and Kim review: "As we entered the 1990s, it became suddenly and urgently clear that a tumultuous change was occurring in America and the rest of the world around us. On every front—love, marriage, and the family; religion, politics, and the community; work, leisure, and our global position—the ground beneath our feet began shifting. Yesterday's verities had vanished. Unpredictability and chaos became the norm."[22]

They go on to say that this loss of moral values is the No. 1 problem facing our country.[23] That's the reason William Bennett titled his book *The De-Valuing of America: The Fight for Our Culture and Our Children*. The future of the next generation is at stake. If we lose this culture battle, we have lost the war for civilization. At a symposium in Dallas, 42 Christian youth leaders were asked to state what they saw as the dominant problem of youth today. One hundred percent of them—every single one—said the No. 1 issue was the loss of a biblically based value system.[24]

Think About It

From your own personal memory or your study of history, note how our culture has changed with regard to the following areas since 1960:

1. Lottery, horse racing, riverboat gambling
2. Cheating on exams in high school
3. Social drinking
4. Divorce
5. Premarital and extramarital sex

6. Swearing on television
7. Homosexuality
8. Disrespect for ministers and religion in the media and society
9. Prayer in public school
10. Unborn human life

Drumroll, Please

I wish it were possible for the publisher of this book to implant one of those musical greeting card instruments right here, so that when you turned to this page, you would hear a drumroll. What I'm about to say is just that important. After studying this matter extensively for many years, I am convinced that there is one central issue from which stem all these other social problems we have discussed. Like spokes on a bicycle wheel all coming to one hub, all the moral chaos in our society focuses on one fact. This fact is this: **We have lost our grasp as a nation on what is objectively right and wrong, or even that there is such a thing as objective truth.** A universal standard of right and wrong is the foundational principle upon which all of our moral underpinnings rest. Without that standard, we're building our moral house on the sand. It will wash away with tomorrow morning's tide.

Each of the philosophies discussed in the last chapter had at least one thing in common: the denial of an objective standard of right and wrong. That denial has worked its way into the thinking of our entire society. Research shows that at least 70 percent of baby boomers and generation X do not believe in absolute truth—all truth is relative. The Barna survey of churched teens reflects this conclusion. A majority of these young people did not believe that an objective standard of truth exists. Eighty-five percent agreed with the statement "What is right for one person in a given situation might not be right for another person who encounters the same situation." Seventy-one percent agreed with the statement "When it comes to matters of morals and ethics, truth means different things to different people; no one can be absolutely positive he or she has the truth." Less than 10 percent had a clear view of objective morality.[25] Allan Bloom opens his No. 1 best-seller, *The Closing of the American Mind,* with the following widely quoted observation. Any college professor in America can verify that he is on target with his assessment of today's youth.

There is one thing a professor can be absolutely certain of: almost every student entering the university believes, or says he believes, that truth is relative. If this belief is put to the test, one can count on the students' reaction: they will be uncomprehending. That anyone should regard the proposition as not self-evident astonishes them, as though he were calling into question 2 + 2 = 4. These are things you do not think about. The students' backgrounds are as various as America can provide. Some are religious, some atheists; some are to the Left, some to the Right; some intend to be scientists, some humanists or professionals or businessmen; some are poor, some rich. They are all unified in their relativism.[26]

My experience as a professor in a Christian university yields the same conclusion. Students often tell me that they believe in an objective standard of right and wrong or that they believe the Bible is the final Authority on matters of moral conduct. However, when applied to real-life situations, their choices speak otherwise. Most of them are relativists. And do you know the sad thing? They don't even know it.

I give an interesting assignment to one of my classes composed almost exclusively of baby boomers: students give their definition of truth. Most of them bring God and the Bible into their definition and even quote Jesus' saying, "I am the way, the truth, and the life" (John 14:6, KJV). But not all their answers are examples of orthodoxy. I am surprised at the number of students (at least four in every class) who respond, "Truth is truth when it is truth for me." I thought I was shell-shocked by this frequent response, but just last week a student in one of my classes responded to the question with an answer that made me flinch. He said, "Truth is whatever I want it to be. I define my own truth." Sounds very close to the definitions of truth reached in *The Day America Told the Truth.* Ninety-three percent in that survey said they and they alone decide what is right and wrong for them. The vast majority said they violated both church rules and civil law whenever they wanted. The results of that entire survey are evidence of that fact. The central issue here is objective truth, and many of us in the church don't believe in it.

Again, this doesn't mean we are intentional hypocrites. Hypocrisy has some element of self-awareness in it. I believe we have so successfully compartmentalized our lives into social and religious realms that our right hand honestly does not know what our left hand is doing. That is, our religious vocabulary says one thing ("God gives us an objective standard of right and wrong in the Bible"), but the influences from our culture cause us to think and live quite another way ("All truth is relative"). Thus, we again see that culture is killing us softly.

Here is a recent example from a counseling session I had with one of my students this year. He received disciplinary action from the campus judiciary council and was sent to me for moral counsel. His offense was viewing a pornographic movie in his dormitory room. We had not talked long until I realized our discussion was at a serious impasse. We were thinking on totally different levels.

To summarize his position: he honestly didn't understand why he was being disciplined, why he should admit to doing something wrong, and why he needed to talk to me. He had determined in his mind that this activity was morally correct for him. Why? Because *he* thought so. He agreed that it might not be proper for anyone else, but he could handle the material in the movie. Throughout our conversation he reminded me of how much he loved the Lord and how much he wanted to be involved in leadership positions on our Christian campus. For me the real problem with this student was not that he was caught watching pornography. Rather, it was that he had redefined the rules to the point that he honestly saw absolutely nothing morally questionable about his actions. Unfortunately, this type of reasoning is not isolated among Christians; it is becoming common.

Think About It
1. Why is an objective standard of right and wrong so crucial to the moral underpinnings of a society?
2. What is wrong with moral relativism?
3. Do you or your friends or coworkers entertain notions of a subjective view of truth?
4. What is the final result of a life lived by subjective truth?

Erasing God from the Picture
Objective truth presupposes an objective truth giver, which in turn implies God. Therein lies the problem for our society.

Our popular culture does not want to acknowledge God. If it can effectively erase God from the picture, it can trash objective truth. Then people can make any lifestyle choice and justify it. Our culture has worked hard at making that happen. I would never fault Christians for being a part of this conspiracy. We, for the most part, do not even know it is happening. Our misunderstanding of objective truth is more the *product* rather than the *source* of this cultural move.

Allan Bloom notes that his grandparents were ignorant by our educational standards, but they knew the Bible with its commands and stories. They also knew about objective truth. They lived their lives by the Bible and had a rich spiritual heritage. People in our generation are highly educated, but they do not know the Bible. That is part of the problem. "I mean rather that a life based on the Book is closer to the truth, that it provides the material for deeper research in and access to the real nature of things."[27] The key phrase of that quote is "a life based on the Book." It's not enough to know what the Bible has to say; we know that. We must go on to decide that we are going to make it our authority and abide by its standards.

That is the focus of the next chapter. If we hope to stem the tide of popular culture's influence on our lives and have an impact in the culture war, we must know what the Bible says about objective truth and an objective standard of right and wrong and what Christianity believes in the area of moral principle. Once we have established biblical principles, we can begin to find ways to apply them to our lives and bring our conduct in line with our beliefs.

5

Here We Stand

What Christians Believe
About Making Moral Choices

Teacher's Gone

One of the most valuable lessons I ever learned in childhood came my way one fall day when I was in the sixth grade. The lesson dealt with my understanding of rules, social control, and authority. Our teacher, who had to be out of the classroom for a while, left us with an assignment to be completed in her absence. To that point in my young life I had had no awareness of any personal hostility toward authority. However, the minute our teacher left the room and closed the door behind her, the entire classroom was transformed almost magically into a world of chaos. Students exploded in frenzied activity; I was positioned in the big middle of it. I knew there was a time and a place for free expression, and this was it! Everything happened but work on our assignment.

At the height of the pandemonium, one of the girls in class interrupted the festivities with "You guys had better get quiet and work on your assignment!" Our quick and clever response was "Oh yeah? What are *you* going to do about it?" Her reply stopped us dead in our tracks, like hitting the pause button on a VCR: "The teacher appointed me to take names, and when she gets back, I'm going to show her this." She held up a piece of paper with all our names on it. She had our attention!

The dust settled quickly, and we all went to work on our assignment. The whispering that followed focused on how we could save our necks and salvage our deportment grade for that grading period. Everybody was sweating—everybody but me, that is. I remained as cool as a cucumber. Why was I so self-assured? Because the girl taking names was my cousin. Family loyalty has its privileges! I was certain Marlyn would not turn my name in with the other rabble-rousers. I couldn't have been more wrong. In fact, after that day I vowed that Marlyn's name would not appear in my will—provided I lived long enough to write one.

The teacher returned. Marlyn turned in her list. We were all in big trouble! Our parents received a note from the teacher about our short-but-sweet experiment with anarchy. I don't remember what happened at any of my friends' houses, but I surely remember what happened at mine. Time to write a will was definitely out of the question! I got one of those lectures in which your parents call you "Mister" and use your middle name. I was grounded until further notice.

That event made an obvious impact on my life. More than 30 years have passed, but the memory is as fresh as if it had happened yesterday. The lesson learned remained: when the authority figure is absent and can't see our actions, and when chances are favorable that we won't be held accountable, we're prone to do just about anything we want to do. Lawlessness lurks just below the surface.

Let's Suppose

Applying that insight to the subject of this book, let me take you on a mental odyssey for a moment. Suspend for a few minutes what you know to be true, and engage with me in free-thinking speculation.

- First, let's suppose that there is no God, or at least no one to whom we must answer.
- Second, suppose that there is no such thing as intrinsic right or wrong. No universal norms govern human conduct; no objective standards exist as a rule of thumb to direct human behavior. Since there is no God, you do not have a Moral Governor to uphold such rules anyway. You need not have rules if you don't have a rule enforcer. As Russian philosopher Fyodor Dostoyevsky put it, "If God is dead, everything is permitted."
- Third, suppose there is no purpose for human existence. All life on the earth resulted from a chance collision of

various elements and over a very long period of time evolved upward to the variety of life we now know. This life includes plants, water creatures, land animals, and humanity. We acknowledge that all of these exist because we have evidence of them all around us. What we deny is that there is any *purpose* for their existence. Living beings just happen to exist.

- Fourth, suppose that there are no lasting consequences for any of our actions. Since we have no rules, we are free to do whatever we want to do. Since God does not exist, we need not worry about having to answer ultimately for anything that we think, say, or do. Do whatever you want.

Does this hypothetical situation sound far-fetched to you? It shouldn't. It is the worldview and the perception of reality for the majority of people living in our society today. No involvement by God, no rules, no authority, no consequences. It sounds like a perfect formula for moral anarchy, does it not? It sounds like a good explanation for why our society is in its current moral condition.

Think About It

Be totally honest with yourself for a moment. Don't write anything down; just think about it. Answer these two questions:

1. If in the depths of your heart you believed the hypothetical situation above to be an accurate reflection of reality, would you live your life any differently than you do right now?
2. What are three reasons that you would or would not live differently?

   a.

   b.

   c.

I have asked these questions dozens of times in dozens of different settings. I always get the same answer. Most people would live differently. So don't think you're unique if you answered the first question positively.

Look back over the hypothetical situation I proposed above. Can you think of reasons that so many people in our society think this way? While we may not have the definitive answer, there are some possible reasons.

The idea of no God or an uninvolved God comes to us from

secular humanism. A review of the *Humanist Manifesto II* shows atheism as a central feature of this position. Humanists are at every level of society lobbying for their positions. They have been fairly effective in their efforts at indoctrination.

The absence of universal norms comes to us from pluralism. This position asks, "How can any one person's ideas or an entire system of thought be judged as superior to another?" All views are equally acceptable. Thus, no objective standards of right and wrong can exist.

The lack of purpose in human existence comes from the teachings of naturalistic evolution. The theory of survival of the fittest needs no purpose for life on this earth. Everything is the result of random chance, according to this position.

The lack of lasting consequences is a frequent theme on television. Our society sees literally thousands of scenes of sexual intimacy between nonmarried people on television each year. Almost never are these relationships portrayed as having the consequences of guilt, heartache, pregnancy, disease, broken relationships, or even death, as with AIDS. This example of the absence of consequences could be multiplied by almost every moral choice that television misrepresents.

A Solid Foundation

Those of us who are Christians have a very strong conviction that this hypothetical situation is, in fact, not a true reflection of reality. We believe that certain facts and principles govern and describe the nature of reality on this earth. The purpose of this chapter will be to present some of the facts and principles that relate to making moral choices. In order to do this, we must have a point of reference that becomes the authority for our position. Without such a point of reference, we have no foundation upon which to base our lifestyle choices.

The most popular points of reference in our world today are personal reason, personal experience, and an appeal to human nature. Philosophers for the last several hundred years have noted the limits of human reason. At best, we never have all the facts, and we don't have flawless reasoning ability. Therefore, reason alone doesn't make a good authority for moral choices.

Personal experience is also flawed as a base of authority, since no one has had enough experiences to give insight into every possible moral choice. How many times have people said to me, "If I knew then what I know now, I never would have done it"? Both personal reason and personal experience are relative authority bases. They are as different and varied as the number of people using them. They yield different definitions of right and wrong based on who is using them.

An appeal to human nature assumes that people will do the right thing when they know what is right. Such an appeal sounds lofty, but a quick review of today's newspaper proves that it's not true. Many people have more moral awareness than they are living. Ethical philosophers are incorrect if they assume "To know right is to do it."

Christians seek an authority base for moral choices in something deeper than personal reason, personal experience, or human nature. We presuppose that a revelation from God to humanity on these matters is found in the Bible. We should never be ashamed that we have presuppositions. *Everybody* has them. We all start our thought process with concepts and perceptions that we cannot prove.

We believe the Bible presents an accurate understanding of God, a created order for the universe, and His purpose and plan for humanity. We believe the Holy Spirit of God spoke to the writers of Scripture in such a clear manner that they accurately recorded a revelation from God powerful enough to be called "the Word of God." The Spirit of God watched over the transmission of this Word from generation to generation and language to language, so that we can be assured that our present translation of Scripture in our particular language accurately represents what God said to the original writers. We further believe the Holy Spirit illuminates our minds to understand this revelation of God in the Bible when we read it with eyes of faith.

So the Holy Spirit was involved in the creation and transmission of Scripture and now is involved in the explanation of God's Word to our hearts. Because we believe this to be true, we affirm that the Bible has the ultimate authority to define the meaning of life, reality on this earth, and how we should conduct our lives. In fact, it is final Authority for all that is true and right.

If you believe these presuppositions about the Word of God, then we can go on to unlock what the Bible says about everything in the moral order of the world. If you don't believe in the authority of the Bible, then we have no point of reference upon which to continue our discussion—discussion ended, class dismissed.

In defining Christian principles for making moral choices, we must set the foundation upon which we can build our entire worldview. We'll start with the basics to assure a solid foundation. Each foundation block is a central feature of our faith. For some readers this will be new information; for most it will be review. If it's review for you, try to read it with new eyes, and let these truths sink deeply into your mind. I find that it's good for me to review these truths myself occasionally to keep my Christian perspective clearly focused. We hear such a conflicting message from the world on a daily basis that it sometimes becomes tempting to entertain the notion that they might be correct. We must again affirm these Christian truths as we contemplate making lifestyle choices.

Foundation Block 1: God exists. This is an unproved and unprovable presupposition we bring to the discussion. Occasionally students come to me with Bible in hand and say, "I'm trying to convince a friend of the reality of God. Show me proof of God's existence in the Bible." They look at me as if I've lost my mind when I reply, "I can't. The Bible doesn't attempt to prove God's existence. It takes it for granted as a logical assumption of life." The Bible begins with "In the beginning *God*" (Gen. 1:1, emphasis added) and goes on from there. It urges us to observe our natural surroundings, life, and ourselves and postulate one good reason why we should *not* believe in God. As Ps. 14:1 reads, "The fool says in his heart, 'There is no God.'"

Foundation Block 2: God created the physical universe and humanity with purpose and declared that it is good. (See Gen. 1—2, especially 1:31—"God saw all that he had made, and it was very good.") God remains separate from His creation, in opposition to the pantheism of our day, which teaches that God blends His being with nature and becomes one with His universe. He also remains above His creation in that He does not depend upon it for personal identity or fulfillment. God carefully planned all that He created. None of the created order happened by random chance. It is ordered and orderly; all is here for a reason. This gives God's creation purpose. We deny the naturalism of our day, which teaches that everything just happens to be this way.

Because God made everything, matter and the created order are not inherently evil. We obviously see evil in our world, but it is not the fault or the plan of God. He also actively sustains His creation on a daily basis. This means that we deny the deistic view of God that removes Him from the daily sustenance of all things. He is not an absentee landlord.

Foundation Block 3: God establishes truth, which His very nature defines. Jesus said in John 14:6, "I am the way and *the truth* and the life" (emphasis added). This reminds us that truth exists in our world because Jesus is involved in our world. Some facts and principles are true, and others are false—objectively true or false. It sounds very elementary. Yet from everything we have seen thus far, we know that this foundation block is not accepted by a majority of people in our society. All that is true about our world comes from God. We cannot compartmentalize truth into "scientific truth" and "religious truth," for example. Only one truth exists. If something is true, it is God's truth.

Foundation Block 4: God has knowledge of everything we do and say, as well as our thoughts, attitudes, desires, and motives. Further, He is keeping record of it all. First Chron. 28:9 reminds us, "The LORD searches every heart and understands every motive behind the thoughts." Ps. 94:11 says, "The LORD knows the thoughts of man."

Where do you suppose God is recording all this information? Much speculation has been offered. Some think God has a giant computer in heaven on which He is recording everything; others say He has perfect memory. I don't know where God is storing this information, but I do know where *we* store it. Medical scientists tell us that every action, word, thought, feeling, motivation, attitude, and intention that we have ever had for every day of our lives is permanently stored in our brains. We know this is true through use of our memory. God has a record of our lives—and so do we.

Foundation Block 5: We will stand before God and give an account of our lives to Him on Judgment Day. Second Cor. 5:10 reminds us, "For we must all appear before the judgment seat of Christ, that each one may receive what is due him for the things done while in the body, whether good or bad." All information about us is recorded for God to access, except for one important omission. Everything for which we have asked God's forgiveness is deleted! That information is covered by the blood of Jesus Christ because of our faith in Him. "As far as the east is from·the west, so far has he removed our transgressions from us" (Ps. 103:12). Also remember Mic. 7:19: "You will again have compassion on us; you will tread our sins underfoot and hurl all our iniquities into the depths of the sea." God has all the information and the reasoning necessary to make a proper judgment. Jesus Christ will be our impartial Judge (John 5:22: "Moreover, the Father judges no one, but has entrusted all judgment to the Son"). We will be judged to spend eternity in either heaven, with its boundless rewards, or hell, with its boundless punishments.

Selective Listening

We've not said all that could be said about the Christian faith as it lays a foundation for moral conduct. That would constitute an entire systematic theology book in itself. However, we have enough information before us to begin construction of a Christian perspective on right behavior. It is important that we believe *all* that the Bible has to say to us on this subject. The popular notion of our day is not to abandon the Bible and religious faith entirely, but to practice selective listening.

In Reginald Bibby's *Fragmented Gods,* he reports that Canadians are not abandoning their religious faith. They know what traditional Christianity believes, and they still want to be numbered in the ranks. But they're fragmenting their beliefs to keep what they want to believe, adjust what they want to change, add what they want to incorporate from cultural and other religious sources, and discard what doesn't work for them. It's like a religious buffet—religion à la carte with a smorgasbord of fragmented choices. We're doing exactly the same thing worldwide. Bibby says, "For some time now, a highly specialized, consumer-oriented society has been remolding the gods. . . . The problem with all of this is that religion, instead of standing over against culture, has become a neatly packaged consumer item—taking its place among other commodities that can be bought or bypassed according to one's consumption whims. Religion has become little more than a cultural product and is coming precariously close to acknowledging that culture creates the gods."[1] We must guard against selective listening but must hear all the Bible has to say to us about right conduct.

Think About It

1. What are some ways you have practiced selective listening with your parents, friends, or mate?
2. What was the nature of the subject matter you didn't want to hear or acknowledge?
3. What are some ways we may practice selective listening with God's Word?
4. Why do you suppose it's becoming popular to fragment our Christian beliefs?

God Is . . .

A proper understanding of God is absolutely essential if we are to have a true picture of reality. A proper understanding of God is also essential for a proper perspective on our conduct. One of the observations of social scientists is that a society tends to become like the god or gods it serves. We take on a resemblance of our god. As A. W. Tozer says, "It is impossible to keep our moral practices sound and our inward attitudes right while our idea of God is erroneous or inadequate. . . . A right conception of God is basic . . . to practical Christian living."[2] This point is clearly illustrated in the decadent lifestyle of ancient Greece and Rome as it followed the lead of its immoral gods and goddesses. The same was true in biblical times with the Hebrew people's neighbors, the Canaanites. God tried to keep His chosen people away from the immoral culture and lifestyle choices of these heathen people who worshiped Baal.

The Christian God is a personal being, not an impersonal force at work in the world. Many world faiths serve an impersonal deity; Christianity is different. Our God is a person with a name and a personality like you and me. Some of the names for God given in the Bible include El, El Shaddai, Adonai, Yahweh, Elohim, and I Am; each name relates different features of His personality. In Exod. 3:14 we read, "God said to Moses, 'I AM WHO I AM. This is what you are to say to the Israelites: "I AM has sent me to you."'" He also has personal qualities that define and describe Him as a person. Entire books have been written about the attributes or personal qualities of God. A proper understanding of all His attributes is essential to a proper relationship with Him. Unfortunately, space does not permit a discussion of each of them here, though several will be mentioned.

---◆---

Christian Principle: *God is a person with a personality.*

---◆---

One of these is holiness. God is a holy being. The concept of holiness is one of the major features of the Bible, used more than 830 times. Sometimes God's holiness is described in the Hebrew language as a bright light. "Who among the gods is like you, O LORD? Who is like you—majestic in holiness, awesome in glory, working wonders?" (Exod. 15:11). At other times He is presented as being separate from everything that is unholy. "'To whom will you compare me? Or who is my equal?' says the Holy One" (Isa. 40:25). Sometimes God's holiness is pictured as purity. Isaiah's vision of God in 6:1-13 pictures Him as a God of purity. As A. W. Tozer puts it, "Holy is the way God is. To be holy He does not conform to a standard. He is that standard."[3]

We cannot underestimate the holiness of God. It is the central characteristic from which all others flow—the sum total of His essence. It is the most important single attribute of God, both in the number of biblical references and in biblical emphasis about the character of God. God's purity is an absolute purity, unstained by evil. Habakkuk says to God, "Your eyes are too pure to look on evil; you cannot tolerate wrong" (1:13). The Bible tells us not only that our God is a holy God but also that He expects the same of us. That's why the Bible so often connects God's holy character with a call to uprightness in our conduct. Lev. 20:26 reads, "You are to be holy to me because I, the LORD, am holy, and I have set you apart from the nations to be my own." (See also Matt. 5:48.) Second Cor. 6:17 reminds us, "Therefore come out from them and be separate, says the Lord. Touch no unclean thing, and I will receive you." This call to separation from the world is a biblical requirement for our holiness. However, separation alone does not guarantee our holiness. The holiness God requires of us comes to us only as we make ourselves available for Him to share His holiness with us. It is a result of His grace in us.

———◆———

Christian Principle: *God is holy and expects the same of us.*

———◆———

A discussion of God would not be complete without speaking of His great love. Biblical images and references abound telling of God's love for us. He presents himself to us as our Heavenly Father (Exod. 4:22; Deut. 1:31). Moses reminded the Hebrew people that everything in the universe belongs to God, yet He has set His affection on us and lavished us with His love (10:14-15). A beautiful representation of God's love for us is the life example of the prophet Hosea. Read this Old Testament book again, and see God's love reaching out to us. The most amazing and incomprehensible expression of God's love comes in the gospel message of sending His Son Jesus Christ to tell us personally about that love and then to die on the Cross for our sins. Unbelievable love! John beautifully summarizes it: "For God so loved the world that he gave his one and only Son, that whoever believes in him shall not perish but have eternal life. For God did not send his Son into the world to condemn the world, but to save the world through him" (John 3:16-17).

Other descriptions of God's characteristics that contribute to our understanding of His greatness include the following:

- Unlimited and illimitable. Nothing in the created order can make such a claim (Job 11:7).
- Present everywhere at once without having to travel from here to there (Ps. 139:7-12).
- Unrestrained by time. He is aware of the past, present, and future at once (Matt. 28:19-20).
- Perfectly knowledgeable of all facts (Ps. 147:5).
- All-powerful to do anything in keeping with His nature and will (Phil. 3:21).
- Sovereign over the entire universe (Deut. 4:39).
- Constant in nature, changing neither quantitatively nor qualitatively with the changing circumstances of life on earth (Ps. 102:26-27).
- Righteous to do always what is right and proper (Ps. 145:17).

- Just to judge everyone and all circumstances fairly and impartially (Ps. 97:2).
- Gracious to give us what we do not earn or deserve (Eph. 2:7-9).
- Merciful not to give us the punishment we justly deserve (Matt. 9:35-36).
- Truthful to represent things accurately (Titus 1:2).
- Faithful to keep all His promises (1 Thess. 5:24).
- Persistent to offer us His salvation throughout life (2 Pet. 3:9).

What an awesome picture of God! I could think for hours about each of these characteristics. They truly boggle the human mind. A complete picture of God will ever remain incomprehensible. We are creatures; He is the Creator. We cannot possibly contain Him in our thinking. However, we know enough to realize how He expects us to live, love, and serve Him.

Think About It

Look over the list of the characteristics of God, and answer the following questions:
1. Which characteristic do you find most inspiring?
2. Which characteristic do you find most comforting in time of trouble?
3. Which characteristic do you find hardest to grasp?
4. Which characteristic is the greatest help to you?

In His Image

Foundation Block 2 stated: "God created the physical universe and humanity with purpose and declared that it is good." He made humanity special by creating us in His image. We are uniquely higher than all other created realities on the earth. Nature is our sister, not our mother. We are to respect and care for it, but not to worship it. Ps. 8:5 reminds us, "You made him [humanity] a little lower than the heavenly beings and crowned him with glory and honor." The image of God implies a variety of qualities, such as an ability to love, communicate, and relate to others; intelligence or reasoning ability; a moral component or knowledge of right and wrong; a free will to make moral choices; spiritual life with the option for eternal life; and authority over creation.

The crowning feature of God's image in us is that we have a capacity for fellowship with Him. The fullest expression of God's image in us comes only through personal relationship with Him, our original intended purpose. That is when our communication is at its best. No human telecommunication linkup will ever equal our ability to talk with the Almighty Creator of the universe. All of God's creation is of worth and value, but we are qualitatively different and have a qualitatively different worth. Even though this image has been marred and damaged by sin, it has not been destroyed. It exists and functions well enough to remind us that we were made to know, love, and obey God. We will never find true satisfaction in life unless we live in relationship with Him.

God placed His image in us, not only so we could communicate with Him, but also so we could be His representatives on this earth. We are to show the world how God wants people to live by the way we ourselves live. We can do this effectively only as we live close to Him and remain dependent upon Him. His enabling power makes it possible for us to represent Him well. Relationship remains the key.

—◆—

Christian Principle: *Because we are in the image of God, we can have personal relationship with Him.*

—◆—

Is That Right?

It doesn't matter that 70 percent of the citizens of the United States don't believe in the validity of objective truth. God's Word says that truth exists in our world, and no opinion poll will ever change that. Norman Geisler in his book *Christian Ethics* offers a number of ways our world defines what is right:

1. Right is determined by the one with the most power.
2. Right is determined by your social group.
3. Right is determined by your own personal choice.
4. Right is determined by the whole human race.
5. Right is determined by using moderation.
6. Right is determined by giving yourself pleasure.
7. Right is determined by seeking good for the most people.
8. Right is determined by what is desirable for its own sake.
9. Right cannot be determined.
10. Right is determined by God's will.[4]

As Christians we obviously opt for the last one. We must recapture the notion in our own personal lives and for our society that some things are true and others false. It may not be popular, and it may not be politically correct, but God says that's the way it is. It may be popular to ride the fence of uncertainty, no judging of others, and tolerance, but that's not where God wants us to be. His is a call to come down off the fence and take our stand with Him on the side of objective truth. If we don't, He will stand alone, because He will not deny the truth (Deut. 32:4; John 18:37; Rom. 3:4).

—◆—

Christian Principle: *God is the Author of objective truth.*

—◆—

God established the moral order of our world with universal norms or objective standards of right and wrong. This is a logical conclusion from Foundation Block 3: "God establishes truth, which His very nature defines." Moral order exists in our world by divine moral law the way physical order exists by physical law. Physical laws such as gravity and inertia give our world predictability and reliability. We can defy these laws if we choose, but we cannot invalidate them. The same is true with God's moral laws, which give our world moral reliability. People may not always choose to follow these moral laws, but they cannot invalidate them.

—◆—

Christian Principle: *God establishes the moral order of our world.*

—◆—

Because of objective truth, some courses of action are right in God's eyes, and others are wrong. Regardless of the situation or the individuals involved, circumstances and personalities do not alter the parameters of universal norms. What is wrong in God's eyes today will be wrong tomorrow. What is wrong for all humanity does not find its exception with me and my desires. Opinion polls don't change the boundaries. Even if every person in the world decided to adopt a particular course of action, it would not change God's pronouncement on the matter. Universal norms are hardwired into the created order. Moses began his presentation of the Ten Commandments with "And

God spoke all these words" (Exod. 20:1, emphasis added). That makes it final for Christians. Thus, we deny the relativism, subjectivism, and situationism of our culture.

Truth is not fluid or moldable like soft putty. My student was incorrect when he said, "Truth is whatever I want it to be." It is *not* whatever we want it to be. We may deceive one another and ourselves until we all believe it, but the definition of truth remains the same. It has always been more popular to exchange the truth of God for a lie (Rom. 1:25). We humans have been doing that since the Garden of Eden.

———◆———

Christian Principle: *God gives us objective standards of right and wrong.*

———◆———

Why is truth constant and universal rather than relative and subjective? Because the definition of truth has its roots in the nature of God himself, who is the Source of all truth. This is so strongly the case that the Holy Spirit is often referred to as "the Spirit of Truth." In order to be in touch with truth, we must be in touch with the Spirit of God. This is the reason our society has drifted so far from a grasp of truth—it has drifted away from God. John 16:13 says, "But when he, the Spirit of truth, comes, he will guide you into all truth." (Read also 14:17; 15:26; and 1 John 4:6.) When God shows us genuine truth as only He fully knows it, we then begin to understand the true nature of things and see clearly as He helps us to see.

The philosophers are correct when they say our world is in constant change. The only thing for sure is that everything is changing. This is not true of God and His truth, however. Both God and truth remain constant and unchanging with the changes of circumstances and time.

Truth is not only something we know in our minds but also something we live through God's power. John 3:21 declares, "But whoever lives by the truth comes into the light, so that it may be seen plainly that what he has done has been done through God." With this lifestyle of truth comes freedom from the bondage and enslavement of sin: "You will know the truth, and the truth will set you free" (8:32).

Notice the connection between the previous three sections of this chapter.

1. God is all that is holy and righteous.
2. We are created in His image.
3. God's Word and will define truth.

Therefore, when we choose to live by the truth, there is an alignment of God's image in us with His moral order. We are in touch with our created heritage, so to speak. With that alignment comes freedom.

Think About It

1. How do you believe most of your friends or coworkers determine what is right?
2. Why do you suppose the majority of people struggle with the concept of objective truth?
3. Is it inconsistent for a Christian to have a definition of truth that is relative and subjective? Why or why not?
4. What benefits are there in having a constant God and objective truth in a world that is constantly changing?

Universal Norms

Christian ethics, then, are based on these principles. God, who established the moral order of our world, is the Author of truth with objective standards of right and wrong. We discussed two other types of ethics earlier in the book. A *descriptive ethic* is based on what the majority of people are doing; an *emotive ethic* is based on what people like to do or feel good doing.

Christian ethics represent a third type of ethic: a *normative ethic*. It is based on the Bible, which gives us an objective standard of right and wrong. These objective standards are often called "universal norms." They apply to all people in all places under the same circumstances. They are without exception. They tell us that our actions are inherently good or bad, rather than simply productive of good or bad results. The Ten Commandments (Exod. 20:1-17) are a good example of universal norms. Objective standards of right and wrong are not just based on impersonal commands of God. They flow from His very nature of absolute truth.

Why do you suppose God gave us the Ten Commandments and other universal norms in the Bible? Was it to keep us from having a good time in life? Was it to cramp our style? Most people I know in our society today think the essence of true freedom is the absence of all norms. They resent God for setting up barriers to their free expression. They picture the world like a giant toy store with God as the proprietor, going around placing signs on every toy saying, "Do not play with this." He does this simply to keep us from having a good time, they think.

I believe a more accurate picture is of guardrails at the edge of the Grand Canyon. God doesn't give us universal norms to keep us from having a good time in life; He's trying to save us from heartache and self-destruction. He honestly has our best interests in mind. When we choose to govern our lives by His universal norms, we experience the joy and fulfillment that come only from obeying Him. Again, we don't follow universal norms *because of* the joy and fulfillment we get out of life, although they may follow as a by-product. That would be an end-centered ethic. We do it because we want to live in harmony with God's will and nature, and because we want to live in fellowship with Him.

—◆—

Christian Principle: *God gave universal norms with our best interests in mind.*

—◆—

At this point we could digress into a lengthy discussion that has occupied large amounts of time and volumes of writing on the subject of whether something is right because it is inherently right or it is right because God has declared it to be so. The argument for the latter is that God is powerful enough to define things morally in His world the way He wants to define them. In a quiet moment, contemplate that question. It has interesting ramifications in both directions.

I personally have come to the conclusion that things are right because they are inherently right. I base this belief on the understanding that the nature of God defines the moral order. That which is right in our world lines up with God, who is the very definition of rightness. Therefore, something is right as it squares with the nature of God. God would not go against His own nature and declare something to be right when in reality it is not. These considerations are mentally stimulating, as long as we don't lose the focus of our discussion.

Think About It

1. Why are descriptive and emotive ethics so popular in our culture today?

2. Why do you personally think God gave us universal norms—to cramp our style or to save us grief?
3. Why do most of the people you know think God gave us universal norms—to cramp their style or to save them grief?
4. What difference would it have made to humanity if God had given Moses the "Ten Suggestions" or "Ten Guidelines"?

The Purpose of the Law

It might be beneficial to review the contrasting positions of two great Christian Reformers, Martin Luther and John Calvin, on God's purpose for giving us the Law. Luther believed God gave us the Law to show us how far away from Him and righteousness we are. It serves as a tool of condemnation to point out our guilt and drive us in the direction of God. The problem, however, is that we try to keep the Law by our own strength and fail. This cycle of trying and failing leaves us in constant despair. Calvin, on the other hand, believed God gave us the Law to show us how to live pleasing in His sight. It draws rather than drives. Instead of serving to condemn us, the intention of the Law is to inspire us to come to Christ and do what is right as we are enabled by the Spirit of God.

Luther is correct that the Law shows up our guilt and blame, but I don't believe that is its intended purpose. I agree with Calvin. It is important to remember that God didn't give us the Law as a means of earning His favor. So often Christians and non-Christians alike see the Law in this manner. It is one of the most common misconceptions about Christianity. This is why you observe people trying to follow the universal norms of the Bible before giving their hearts to God and establishing a relationship with Him. They are attempting to earn God's favor by good behavior, such as attending church services and giving up vices. They feel that once they are good enough, they will be worthy to approach God. It is a form of earning favor with Him.

This is the opposite of the way God intends Law and relationship to work. We come to Him and establish a relationship *first*. Then we look to the Law as a way of living to show our gratitude for His mercy upon us. Relationship is prior; the Law follows naturally as a way of saying "Thank You" to God. The Bible presents God entering into covenantal relationships with Noah (Gen. 9) and Abraham (Gen. 17) long before the Ten Commandments were given (Exod. 20). The Hebrew people were always to see their adherence to the Law as a natural result of their relationship with God. Moses said we are a blessed people just for having this knowledge of how to please God now that we are in relationship with Him: "And what other nation is so great as to have such righteous decrees and laws as this body of laws I am setting before you today?" (Deut. 4:8). It is wonderful that God does not leave us guessing about how to please Him!

—◆—

Christian Principle: *Relationship comes first; the Law follows naturally.*

—◆—

So What Will You Do?

The image of God in humanity gives us the ability to know right from wrong, reasoning ability to discern between the two, and a free will with which to make moral choices. Those are powerful tools! In fact, they are the most powerful things we possess as humans. They are the major features that distinguish us from the animal kingdom. They make us free moral agents (Josh. 24:15; 1 Kings 18:21).

Our Christian belief in free moral agency is in direct opposition to the determinism taught by our society. We do not believe our choices are determined by prior conditioning. We deny that factors outside us and beyond our control have final authority in our lives. We affirm that we have reasoning ability that lifts us above the stimulus response of animals. Most important, we deny the basis for the victim mentality, which is so prevalent in our society today. Human beings are more than pawns in the hands of impersonal deterministic factors of life. We are the highest of God's created beings, and we ought to live like it.

We can use our free moral agency to love and bless God and live pleasing in His sight, or we can use it to curse God and live out of fellowship with Him. What a thought! I am frequently asked by my students why God would give us such potential when He knew we might use it to turn away from Him. I believe He took the risk because He wanted creatures who could love Him freely. If we loved Him out of obligation, we would be nothing more than robots. God cannot have a personal relationship with a world of robots. Love is not true love unless it is a *free* love.

———◆———

Christian Principle: *God gave us a free will so we could love Him freely.*

———◆———

A day never passes without my wife telling me that she loves me. She makes me feel truly loved. But what if the following scene took place at our house? I start to enter the kitchen when I overhear my mother talking with my wife. I stop behind the doorway and listen.

"Did you do it?" Mom asks.

"Yes, I did," replies Sue.

"Then here's your check for $1,000. Now, you keep up the good work. You tell Frank that you love him every day, and there'll be more where that came from."

I'd be crushed. Maybe Sue loves me, and maybe she doesn't. That's not the point. The point is, she's expressing her love out of obligation. I don't want to hear a paid commercial!

The same is true of our relationship with God. He wants our love and our blessing and our moral choices to come from our hearts. So He gives us free moral agency with which to do that. Is there a risk involved? Sure. Is it worth that risk? God thinks so, and so do I.

Not So Fast

It may appear, from what we have said in the previous sections, that we have all the components necessary for righteous moral lifestyle choices. We have established the principles of God, moral order, objective standards of right and wrong, and free moral agency. Does it not follow a simple line of logic that all we have to do is make up our minds to do what is right, then do it? Not exactly. If that were the case, I could just make a simple statement like "You know what's right—so do it," and this chapter would be ended. Unfortunately, it's not that easy. We still need to consider one more important feature of the Christian perspective.

I mentioned that God created our first parents with free moral agency. I failed to mention that they used their free wills to disobey Him. The events of Gen. 3 regarding the fall of humanity are as well known as any biblical story. Adam and Eve's choice to place their wills above God's will and satisfy their desire for self-rule created three problems on the human scene. First, it introduced acts of sinning into human history and broke our fellowship with God. Second, it inclined human nature toward self-gratification; theologians call this "original sin." Third, it corrupted earthly systems away from God and godliness; theologians call this "systemic evil." The net result on humanity is profound.

Let's suppose I'm in a situation in which I must choose between doing one thing or another. I already prefer one of the choices in my affections and thinking. I know from my ability to discern right from wrong that the thing I prefer is wrong as established by God's objective standards. Both choices are before me. Is this an evenly balanced selection? No, because three votes have already been cast for the wrong thing:

1. Many people all around me, including most of my friends, have opted for self-preference, like Adam and Eve. Their examples have a powerful influence.
2. The systems of this world (social, political, economic, and so on) favor the wrong choice. They will even give me extra points at work and in my social standing if I choose their way.
3. I have an internal inclination for the wrong thing. I don't know why, but the choice just feels so good; how could it be wrong?

---◆---

Christian Principle: *The pessimism of sin paints a dark picture.*

---◆---

It is almost as if I am doomed to failure before I make my choice. Why bother? Sounds pretty hopeless, does it not? That's why this situation is called "the pessimism of sin." It's a dark picture indeed. However, it's not the whole picture.

Think About It

Think of a time when you had to choose between right and wrong and you chose the wrong.

1. Did it feel as if the two choices were evenly balanced, or did the wrong decision have more appeal?

2. What influences or examples did you have in the wrong direction?
3. How strong was the impression that you should do right, regardless of your personal desire?

The Rest of the Picture

God was not caught off guard by humanity's choice to sin against Him. Before the Father created the world and placed humanity upon it, He had a plan that made provision to bring sinners back to himself through the sacrifice of His Son, Jesus Christ. Rev. 13:8 speaks of "the Lamb [Jesus Christ] that was slain from the creation of the world." Paul speaks of God's grace being "given us in Christ Jesus before the beginning of time" (2 Tim. 1:9). That is the gospel message we read throughout the New Testament.

The word "gospel" means "good news." The good news is that God had a plan to forgive us of our acts of sinning, restore our broken relationship with Him, break sin's power in our lives, and enable us to live righteously. All this is possible through His grace as we are made right in His eyes when we confess our sins, ask forgiveness, and have simple faith in His Son Jesus. This is the rest of the picture; the pessimism of sin is counterbalanced by the optimism of God's grace. The darkness gives way to the light of God's love for us—a love so strong that He willingly sacrificed His Son for us (John 3:16-17).

—◆—

Christian Principle: *The optimism of God's grace changes the picture from darkness to light.*

—◆—

Not on Your Own

Most people, Christian and non-Christian alike, have an innate awareness that it is more desirable to do what is right than to do what is wrong. Most people also wish they could do what is right, even though their definitions of right and wrong are not always biblical. However, most non-Christians and even many Christians don't think it is practically possible to avoid the wrong and do the right consistently. They feel we are doomed to failure by the very definition of our humanness. In their way of thinking, our humanness sets us up for certain defeat. They believe it is theoretically impossible for us to live lives of righteousness.

This mode of thinking is partially right but mostly wrong. It is correct that we cannot consistently avoid the wrong and do the right by using our free will alone. The three votes cast against us that we discussed previously are powerful influences. The Fall did not make our physical being inherently evil, as some say. However, it did damage our situation to the point that we are unable to live righteous lives by our own power and ability. We have neither the consistency of will nor the moral and spiritual strength to do so.

This is another point at which the grace of God sheds optimistic light on our human condition. More good news—God does not expect us to do it on our own! The same grace that forgives us of sin and saves us from sinning also keeps us from sin. The power and ability come to us as a gift from God when we ask in faith. This completes the picture for Christians. The Spirit of God gives us the ability to discern right from wrong, the desire to do what is right, and the ability to live it consistently on a daily basis. It is the benefit of God's grace at work in us from start to finish.

What I have quickly summarized in the last two sections is the two aspects of God's grace. First, God showed grace toward us by sending His Son (Rom. 3:24). Second, God places grace within us as He empowers us to live righteously before Him (Phil. 1:11).

---◆---

Christian Principle: *God's grace gives us the power to live pleasingly in His sight.*

---◆---

Several years ago Sue and I counseled a young lady who struggled with her lifestyle choices. She had been raised by a Christian mother and knew the difference between right and wrong. However, she consistently chose to do wrong. She was defeated and miserable. The mental barrier through which she seemingly could not break was this liberating message of the gospel, that God has enabling grace to help us do what is right. Read Eph. 1:3-14 for Paul's summary of God's plan to make us successful in righteous living. Paul reminds us of the entire scope of God's salvation efforts in sending Jesus Christ to die for us and the Holy Spirit to live in us. I wish I could say that our friend broke through that barrier and found the grace of God adequate for her life, but she did not. Unfortunately, as long as we knew her, she remained in bondage to a mind-set of defeat.

Sowing and Reaping

One of the principles of life is that our actions have consequences. This is true for both good and bad behavior. Gal. 6:7-8 remind us, "Do not be deceived: God cannot be mocked. A man reaps what he sows. The one who sows to please his sinful nature, from that nature will reap destruction; the one who sows to please the Spirit, from the Spirit will reap eternal life."

Consequences come in at least two forms. Sometimes they are built into a course of action, mere cause and effect. For example, abuse of our bodies through smoking, drinking, overeating, and so on has a detrimental effect, making us more susceptible to disease. Some of these built-in consequences actually get into social systems and plague our family lineage. This is clearly seen in the effects of an alcoholic person on his or her children and grandchildren. Counselors remind us of the devastating effects upon several generations. This is the meaning of Exod. 20:5: "punishing the children for the sin of the fathers to the third and fourth generation of those who hate me." It is also the message of Ezek. 18:2: "The fathers eat sour grapes, and the children's teeth are set on edge." It is not that God is choosing to punish future generations for someone else's sins, but that natural consequences will run their course.

Another type of consequence is imposed by God acting as Moral Governor of the universe. These consequences come both in this life and at the Final Judgment. We believe God is actively involved in our world, both sustaining nature and working actively in the lives of individuals. He grants us health and safety and watches over our lives in more ways than we will ever know this side of eternity. Therefore, it should not surprise us that, like any loving parent, God punishes us when we disobey His law and do what we know to be wrong. His intention is to correct us and get us back on the right track, not to harm us (Ezek. 33:11; Hos. 6:1; Rev. 3:20). The ultimate consequences for our behavior, however, will come at the Final Judgment.

———◆———

Christian Principle: *Our actions have consequences.*

———◆———

Judgment Day

Our society takes issue with many of our Christian beliefs and principles. None of our doctrines offend it more than talk of the Day of Judgment, when we will all stand before God and give an account of our lives. Humanists and naturalists think we die like animals and simply cease to exist. Universalists think we all automatically go to heaven, because God is too loving to judge us and send some to a place of punishment. Moreover, our society places so much emphasis on living in the here and now that little if any consideration is given to making preparation for eternity.

———◆———

Christian Principle: *We will stand before God and give an account of our lives on Judgment Day.*

———◆———

Many people in our society today don't want to be reminded of God's judgment. The emphasis in our day is on a God of love. Indeed, God is the very definition of love. Nonetheless, He is a God of justice, the Moral Governor of the universe. He must ultimately right the wrongs of this world. On Judgment Day the truth will be revealed about all circumstances and events on this earth. Accounts will be settled once and for all. The purpose of discussing the Judgment is not to scare people, but to give them confidence. First John 4:17 reads, "In this way, love is made complete among us so that we will have confidence on the day of judgment, because in this world we are like him."

Even so, our world still resists any thoughts of ultimate consequences for our actions. I attended a conference of ministers and college professors a couple of years ago in which a lawyer addressed our group. He told of a situation involving a lady who visited a church one Sunday morning and heard a sermon on Judgment Day. The woman was brought under conviction by the Spirit of God. She responded by suing the church for mental distress. She won and bankrupted the congregation. No doubt some ministers have sensationalized their message with "hellfire and damnation preaching." But our response should not be to soft-pedal the Christian message into a more politically correct form. That will not change the Word of God.

I cautioned earlier about the danger of selective listening. If I took the popular or convenient route at this point, I would skip over this entire subject. Perhaps no topic is more sensitive among Christians than this discussion of Judgment Day. However, if we believe in the authority of Scripture, there's no way around it. God's Word plainly teaches that we will stand before the judgment bar of God and give an account of our lives. Heb. 9:27 reminds us, "Man is destined to die once, and after that to face judgment." Other references to the Day of Judgment include Matt. 25:31-32; 2 Pet. 2:9; 3:7; Jude 14-15; Rev. 22:12.

Rev. 20:12 reads, "And I saw the dead, great and small, standing before the throne, and books were opened. Another book was opened, which is the book of life. The dead were judged according to what they had done as recorded in the books." The account of our lives will include not only our words and actions but also, as Foundation Block 4 says, "our thoughts, attitudes, desires, and motives." These latter items are as much a part of who we are as the things we say and do. Jesus tells us in the Sermon on the Mount that He looks beyond our actions to our motives and intentions. For example, "You have heard that it was said to the people long ago, 'Do not murder, and anyone who murders will be subject to judgment.' But I tell you that anyone who is angry with his brother will be subject to judgment" (Matt. 5:21-22).

————◆————

Christian Principle: *Every person who lives on this earth will spend eternity in either heaven or hell.*

————◆————

A presentation on judgment should never have a spirit of harshness or vindictiveness but always a broken heart and an awareness that Christians are dependent upon God's grace as much as anyone. We must never forget 1 Pet. 4:17, which says, "For it is time for judgment to begin with the family of God; and if it begins with us, what will the outcome be for those who do not obey the gospel of God?" After God passes judgment, we will spend an eternity in either heaven or hell.

The Bible gives many characteristics of both heaven and hell. Perhaps the most important feature for us to remember is this: heaven will be blessed with the presence of God; hell will be marked by the total absence of God and all that is good. This is why I am so disturbed by society's flip and casual attitude in its references to hell. For most people, hell describes a bad day at work or a physical problem. We must always remember that our worst day or worst experience on earth cannot even approximate the reality of hell. Neither can our loftiest religious experience capture the glory of heaven. Judgment Day will bring the best and the worst of everything.

Think About It

1. What is the advantage of the belief that when we die we cease to exist?
2. What is the disadvantage of this belief?
3. Why does our culture not like the idea of Judgment Day?
4. Why do many Christians not like the idea of hell?

Here We Stand

On April 18, 1521, at 6 P.M., Martin Luther stood before the officials of the Roman Catholic Church and the German nation to answer charges brought against him for the books he had written criticizing unbiblical teachings and practices in the church. The large assembly hall was packed to capacity; only the emperor could sit. Luther was given an opportunity to recant his teachings and save his position in the church. It would have been much easier for him to back down and give in to social pressure. But Martin Luther was a man of integrity. So with every eye and ear focused in his direction, he spoke, knowing full well that the implications of his decision might cost him everything.

He said, "My conscience is captive to the Word of God. I cannot and I will not recant anything, for to go against conscience is neither right nor safe. God help me. Amen." Printed versions of the speech summarized his position as "Here I stand. I cannot do otherwise."[5]

Martin Luther remains an example for us nearly 500 years later. Much of what we believe and teach as Evangelical Christians is not met with favor by our society, which is constantly challenging us to recant. We know what the Bible says about

- God's existence and His holiness;
- His purpose and plan for creation;
- truth;
- objective standards of right and wrong;
- free moral agency;
- consequences for our actions;
- final judgment.

We say with Martin Luther, "Our conscience is captive to the Word of God. Here we stand!"

This, then, is what Christians believe about making moral choices. Once we have resolved in our minds that we are going to stand with God and His Word, we are in position to study the biblical text for direction in our daily lifestyle choices. That is the focus of the next chapter.

6

A Lamp and a Light

What the Bible Teaches About
Making Moral Choices

Easy to Assemble

I took a trip through our house the other day and made a mental note of all the items we had purchased across the years that required assembly. Probably half of the things in our house had to be put together. I would love to meet the person who got the bright idea of throwing all the pieces of his or her product into a box and labeling it "Easy to Assemble." Easy for whom? For the one who threw it into the box, of course! If it's so "easy," why not put it together at the factory?

Granted, these "Easy to Assemble" items come with instructions for putting them together, but who can understand the instructions? You need to be an engineer with a Ph.D. to figure out what to do. Those instructions usually make sense to only one person—the one who wrote them! The rest of us just scratch our heads, say "Huh?" a lot, and make up our own directions.

Until a few years ago I didn't need the instructions anyway. I'm not quite sure why. I think it was a "guy thing." When we purchased something that needed to be assembled, I would place all the pieces on the garage floor, take a quick look at everything, and just put it together. Sue would often come out to see how things were going. She would usually pick up the directions and ask, "Don't you need these?" My response was always quick and assured: "Nah. I've got it figured out."

Guys can do that, you know. We have a special circuit in

our brain that allows us to bypass directions. At least that's what I used to think. I started to think otherwise about the hundredth time I got my project all together only to find a few extra pieces under the box. To this day I don't know where some of those pieces were supposed to go. I determined I was home free as long as Sue didn't see them in the back of the garage closet!

Along with my maturity has come the realization that directions are meant to help us. The project usually goes a lot faster, with fewer frustrations and no leftover pieces, when you follow them. That realization has helped me in other areas of my life as well.

Instructions for Life

We established in the last chapter the authority of the Bible as our Foundation for what we believe about making moral choices. All the Christian principles we discussed have their origin in the Word of God. However, the Bible contains much more than these few principles. It is a book of instructions for every area of life.

As much as I have hated getting the directions out and laboring through them, I have learned that in the long run it's the best policy. The same is true with the Bible. It's fairly easy for us to display our Bible in a prominent place in our living room, bedroom, or office. We sometimes even get extra points for bringing our Bible to Sunday School class. But it's another matter entirely for us to open it and search its pages for answers to life's tough problems. Sometimes it's a "pride thing." We don't want to admit that we need help; we like to feel self-sufficient. Sometimes it's a "motivation thing." We want to do it, but not right now. Sometimes it is a "fear thing." We're afraid the Bible will prescribe a plan that will require more of us than we're willing to give. What if God asks too much of me? Nonetheless, when we are honest with ourselves, we'll admit that when it comes to making moral choices, the Bible has the best directions for life we will find anywhere.

A clear illustration of this principle is found in the reform movement of King Josiah in 2 Kings 22—23. The nation of Israel had drifted far from God in their ethical choices and worship. The land was in spiritual decay. King Josiah wanted to get his nation back to God. He began his reform movement by cleaning up and repairing the badly neglected Temple in Jerusalem.

In the process of going through the clutter, Hilkiah the high priest stumbled onto a copy of the Book of the Law (their Bible). He took it to the king, who had it read to the national leaders. Matters had gotten so bad that the people no longer remembered what the Law said. They were shocked when they realized how far they had drifted from the will of God for their lives and their nation. The king gave the order to do whatever was necessary to bring the nation back in line with God's commands. It resulted in a national revival. The important point to remember from this story is that wise moral decisions have their foundation in God's Word. Only His Word gives us a true benchmark by which to judge our lives.

The Bible as Our Guide

This chapter will focus on some of the major themes and passages of Scripture that offer God's help to us in making life's tough choices. The Bible is the Christian's primary Source for guidance in making ethical choices. God gave us a mind with which to think through difficult matters, and He expects us to use our reason. We can consult a fund of information and experience from other Christians who have lived before us. Christian psychologists, sociologists, medical doctors, and ethicists can offer us insight from the latest research. But none of these sources of information in and of themselves give us a Christian ethic.

Ethics cannot be Christian ethics without serious consideration of the Bible. Unfortunately, this chapter is only a thumbnail sketch of what the Bible has to offer. An entire book would be needed to do justice to the effort. This brief chapter is presented to spark your interest and get you started in a deeper study of God's Word as it relates to this whole topic. No doubt you could do personal Bible study for the next year on these passages. I hope you will take the initiative and do just that. Ask your pastor's advice about a trustworthy commentary. Buy a good study Bible. Dig in. Ask for the Holy Spirit's guidance and instruction. Use this chapter as a springboard from which to read God's Word with an eye to seeking biblical principles for making ethical decisions. You'll be amazed at how much help you find.

Before we get to the actual texts, let me make some introductory comments about the Bible as it relates to ethics.

1. We must always remember that the Bible offers us *God's* perspective and will on particular matters. It is not the suggestions of mere humans. The established ethical norms of the Bible are not open to debate. We can accept or reject them, but we cannot change God's mind.

2. Sometimes the Bible offers specific rules on certain courses of action. These are timeless and transcend all cultural manifestations. The Word is very specific about lying, gossiping, stealing, premarital sex, adultery, and a host of other practices. It gives us a precise answer. We do not need to pray to see if God has changed His mind on the matter or if we are an exception to the rule.

3. Sometimes the admonitions of the Bible are conditioned by culture, time, and history. Most of the ceremonial and dietary laws of the Old Testament are not observed by Christians today. Restrictions regarding manner of dress and hairstyle are usually cultural preferences. Jesus did not require His followers to keep these laws. At the Jerusalem Council in Acts 15, the Early Church relieved believers from responsibility to these regulations as well.

4. Some moral issues of our day are not addressed in the Bible. Biomedical ethics, for example, present a new dilemma for us almost every day. Science and technology have opened a whole world of ethical concerns that require a Christian response. These issues did not exist in biblical times. However, the Bible can still give us guidance as we look to the spirit and intent of related issues. For example, while the Bible does not specifically mention abortion, it does uphold the sanctity of human life. While it does not speak against the use of recreational drugs, it does teach that our bodies are the temple of the Holy Spirit.

5. Many of the parables, teaching materials, and Bible characters' life stories have been placed in the Word of God for us to deduce principles of God for living. It is our responsibility to search for the will and purpose of God as we study them. Ethical wisdom and understanding are the fruit of our labor. The Bible is more than a catalog of ethical norms. These principles are just as authoritative as the specific rules found in Scripture, and we are just as responsible for comprehending

and applying these principles to our lives as we are for the specific rules referred to in point 2.

6. When we read the Word of God and diligently apply it to our lives, two things happen. First, Christian character develops. We become more and more like the persons God wants us to become. Second, we develop a sense of certainty about God's will for moral choices. Patterns form that help us become more familiar and comfortable with making godly decisions.

7. We look to Jesus Christ as the perfect Model for all our moral choices. In fact, He is the only perfect Model illustrated for us in the Bible. Every other Bible character made mistakes, sinned, or missed God's will at some point in life. That's why the writer to the Hebrews admonishes us to "fix our eyes on Jesus, the author and perfecter of our faith" (12:2).

With these observations in mind, let us turn to the actual text of the Bible for instruction in making moral choices.

Live with Authority

The Book of Genesis begins at the beginning. Looking at the creation narrative of Gen. 1—2, we see God introducing Adam to the concept of living with authority and rules. Immediately upon placing Adam in the Garden of Eden, the Bible says, "the LORD God commanded the man, 'You are free to eat from any tree in the garden; but you must not eat from the tree of the knowledge of good and evil, for when you eat of it you will surely die'" (2:16-17).

God's command offered immense freedom but forbade one particular action. Adam and Eve had a problem with that one command. The problem was not that it seriously restricted their behavior. Rather, it represented authority over them. We humans from the beginning have had a problem with the concept of authority and being told what we can or cannot do. The first biblical principle, then, for making wise moral choices is that we must submit ourselves to the authority of God and His will for our lives.

On many occasions people have questioned me about a particular moral choice they were in the process of making. They closed their argument with "I know what the Bible says, but I don't see anything wrong with it." Such a statement reflects two attitudes: (1) the superiority of human reason over divine decree and (2) resistance to the authority of God over human will. The bottom line is that we don't like to be told no.

Think About It

1. Why do you think most people don't like to be told what to do?
2. Is it common for your Christian friends or coworkers to want to place their own reason over the authority of God's Word?

Live for Others

Adam and Eve were placed in the garden as husband and wife. God said, "They will become one flesh" (Gen. 2:24; cf. Matt. 19:5). Each had the responsibility of caring for the needs of the other. Marriage teaches us to think of someone other than ourselves and to prefer their needs over ours.

Marriage does not work as God intends if only one person is preferring the other. In that case, only one person is getting his or her needs met. Both must look out for the interests of the other and live in mutual submission. Eph. 5:21 reminds us to "submit to one another out of reverence for Christ." We see this principle taught throughout the Bible, especially in verses 21-33 (see also 1 Pet. 3:1-7). Husbands are often quick to recall Eph. 5:22-24, regarding the wife's obligation, but forget verses 25-28, which tells them to love their wives "just as Christ loved the church and gave himself up for her to make her holy" (vv. 25-26). This biblical principle keeps us from becoming selfish and ingrown in our lifestyle choices.

Think About It

1. In your opinion, how important is it for married people to prefer the needs of their mate?
2. Why does God not want us to be selfish? What's wrong with selfishness?

Look Carefully

The Book of Genesis contains many narratives from the lives of significant figures in salvation history. We read about Noah, Abraham, Sarah, Isaac, Jacob, and Joseph. We see spiritual life at its best and at its worst. We see both good and bad ethical choices. Keep our seventh introductory comment in mind as you study Bible characters: No biblical personality except Jesus Christ is a perfect example.

These people learned as they lived and as salvation history progressed. The revelation of God to humanity was progressive, developing as we comprehended more and more of what God expected of us. Because of their primitive conditions and sometimes barbaric backgrounds, God had to bring these people a long way toward civilized behavior, not to mention ethical purity. Never make excuses for your moral laxity and use a Bible character's failure as justification. When we read between the lines, we see that their actions brought untold grief into their lives and families. Such actions will do the same in your life. The Bible is very frank and open about these matters as a warning so that we might avoid the same mistakes. Examples of such failures include the following:

- Noah getting drunk after the Flood (Gen. 9:20-23)
- Abraham lying to Pharaoh about his relationship with Sarah (Gen. 12:10-20)
- Abraham having a son with Sarah's handmaiden Hagar (Gen. 16:1-4)
- Lot living in wicked Sodom (Gen. 13:10-13; 19:1)
- Lot's daughters getting him drunk so they could seduce him (Gen. 19:30-38)
- Jacob deceiving his brother and father (Gen. 27:1-40)
- Jacob's dysfunctional family with his wives Leah and Rachel (Gen. 29:14—30:24)
- Joseph's insensitivity toward his family in sharing his dreams about ruling over them (Gen. 37:5-11)
- Joseph's scheme of deception to get Benjamin to come to Egypt (Gen. 42:15—43:34)

Why did God continue to work in and through these Bible characters in spite of their shortcomings or failures? Our answer is found in Heb. 11. They lived their lives with faith in God. When they failed, they quickly acknowledged it, asked God's forgiveness, and went on living for Him. Therein lies wise counsel for us. We may fail, but we need not stay defeated. We must seek God's forgiveness and mercy and continue to live our lives with faith in Him.

Think About It

1. Have you ever been tempted to ask why God allowed Old Tes-

tament characters to do things that He will not allow us to do?
2. If so, what kinds of things?
3. What was so impressive to God about Abraham's faith? (Hint—see Rom. 4.)

Sign on the Dotted Line

We discussed in the last chapter the proper sequence of the Law and covenant. The contractual relationship between God and humanity came first; the Law came next as a way of showing gratitude toward Him for that relationship. God sometimes made covenants with individuals like Noah, Abraham, Jacob, and David. He made a covenant with all of humanity when He gave us the Ten Commandments (Exod. 20:1-17). This is a moral contract between God and us. When we become a Christian, we sign our name on the dotted line of this contract and agree to keep its provisions. God agrees to bless and take care of us.

The first four commandments deal with our vertical relationship with God; the remaining six deal with our horizontal relationship with other people. Note that duty to God comes first but does not excuse us from good relations with others. We must balance the two.

- We are to serve only one God.
- We are to avoid all forms of idol worship, which today particularly includes our material possessions.
- We are to avoid using God's name casually or in cursing.
- We are to keep the Sabbath day holy by setting it apart for special time with God and resting from our work.
- We are to honor our parents.
- We are to respect life by not murdering another human being.
- We are to respect our bodies and the marital vows of ourselves and others by not committing adultery.
- We are to respect the property of others by not stealing.
- We are to respect truth and justice by not lying.
- We are to guard our hearts and minds by controlling our desires, attitudes, motives, and intentions by not wanting what belongs to others.

Think About It

1. Why do we need to be in relationship with God before we try to follow His commands?

2. Do you find the Ten Commandments hard or easy to follow? Why?

Be Holy

A significant part of the Law of Moses is the holiness command found in the Book of Leviticus. This book is often difficult to understand because of its culturally bound symbols and expressions. It blends moral and ceremonial law together, making it difficult to discern biblical principles that apply to today. However, the message of holiness clearly underlies all that is said.

One of the most important concepts of Leviticus is the idea of separation. It is both a separation from something and a separation to something. We are to separate ourselves from the mind-set and priorities of the world and separate ourselves to the purposes and person of God. We are to learn His commands and obey them. In so doing, we become more like God. As Lev. 20:26 puts it, "You are to be holy to me because I, the LORD, am holy, and I have set you apart from the nations to be my own." (See also 19:2; 20:7; 21:8; 22:9.)

The holiness message is also found in Deuteronomy. God chose His people and blessed them greatly. Moses said God wanted to continue to bless them. However, they had to stay true to the terms of the contract by living holy lives. The words of Deut. 7:6 reminded Israel and today reminds us, "For you are a people holy to the LORD your God. The LORD your God has chosen you out of all the peoples on the face of the earth to be his people, his treasured possession."

Think About It

1. Name two things you have separated yourself from in order to be holy.
   a.
   b.
2. Name two aspects of God's holiness that you can imitate.
   a.
   b.

Love God

Love for God is highlighted in the Book of Deuteronomy as the primary motivation for keeping His moral laws. We do not obey the law out of slavish obligation but with a child's heart of love. We reverence Him and prefer His ways because we love Him. Sin is not so much breaking God's laws as it is breaking His heart. If we truly love Him, we will not want to hurt Him.

The heart of the message of Deuteronomy is found in 6:4-5. Especially note verse 5: "Love the LORD your God with all your heart and with all your soul and with all your strength." This call to love God is found throughout the book (7:12; 10:12; 11:1, 13, 22; 13:3; 19:9; 30:6, 16, 20). How is it possible for us to love God in this way? Because He gives us an example by the way He loved us first. The message of His love for us is scattered throughout Deuteronomy (5:10; 7:9, 13; 33:3). Though many things are uncertain in this world, one is settled and sure. Never doubt God's love for you. What a powerful motivation for right living!

Think About It

1. What do you see as the major differences between obeying God out of slavish obligation and from a child's heart of love?
2. List three Bible stories that illustrate how much God loves you.

   a.

   b.

   c.

3. If God loves you so much, why does He place moral restrictions on your behavior?

Obey God

Many people think the emphasis of the Old Testament is on meticulously following the letter of the Law without concern for motive or intention. Not so. One of the central messages of the Old Testament is the priority God places on keeping the spirit or intention of the Law and doing it with proper motivation rather than just going through the motions of a ritual with no internal meaning. First Sam. 15:22 emphasizes that priority: "But Samuel replied: 'Does the LORD delight in burnt offerings and sacrifices as much as in obeying the voice of the LORD? To obey is better than sacrifice, and to heed is better than the fat of rams.'" God is not nearly as concerned with our outward religious performance as He is with our heartfelt obedience to His Word and will. Moral behavior from a pure heart always takes precedence over ritual. This is the clear message of the prophets Amos, Hosea, Isaiah, and Micah. Read Amos 5:21-24; Hos. 6:6; Isa. 1:11-17; and Mic. 6:6-8. It is also the message of David in his psalm of confession when he said, "You do not delight in sacrifice, or I would bring it; you do not take pleasure in burnt offerings. The sacrifices of God are a broken spirit; a broken and contrite heart, O God, you will not despise" (51:16-17). The writer of Proverbs captured the essence of the thought when he wrote, "To do what is right and just is more acceptable to the LORD than sacrifice" (21:3).

Jesus made a similar point in Matt. 21:28-31 in His parable of the two sons. Both sons received a request from their father. One paid lip service but did not actually obey. The other resisted at first, then obeyed. Jesus approved of the son who actually obeyed. God's concern is with obedience, not lip service, and with obedience that comes from the desire of our heart to please Him.

Think About It

Think of an example from your religious experience when it was more important to obey God than to perform some religious exercise.

Divine Fellowship

The psalmist David could not find enough ways to adequately express divine-human fellowship. He speaks frequently of the Law of the Lord. In these references he is not referring to the cold, dead letter of the Law, but to the rich, lively fellowship that is enjoyed with God when we follow His Law. It is the door through which we pass to intimate relationship with God. That is the emphasis of David's first psalm, where he says, "Blessed is the man who does not walk in the counsel of the wicked or stand in the way of sinners or sit in the seat of mockers. But his delight is in the law of the LORD, and on his law he meditates day and night" (vv. 1-2). This sweet fellowship is also the reason he prays, "May the words of my mouth and the meditation of my heart be pleasing in your sight, O LORD, my Rock and my Redeemer" (19:14). The nurturing of this divine fellowship is a primary motivation for us to remain sensitive to God's leadership as we make ethical lifestyle choices.

Think About It

What have you found to be the best way to nurture your relationship with God?

Why Do What's Right?

I frequently question my students about the motivation for their right conduct. In other words, why do what's right? Many of our friends in the world are living outside of God's will, and most of them seem to be doing fine. Why should I strive to maintain a righteous life?

The Book of Proverbs gives us two motivations for doing right that serve as the foundation for two types of ethics. The first motivation is because it is the command of God—this leads to an ethic of obligation. The second motivation is because it makes good sense—this leads to an ethic based on good results. Both have merit.

Reverence for God, usually expressed as "the fear of the LORD," is a prerequisite to wisdom (Prov. 1:7; 15:33). Once we have that reverence for God, we become wise and have a proper motivation for obeying His commands. Wisdom does not see the commands of God as restrictive and binding. Rather, it sees them as liberating us to enjoy the best in life; they are "a fountain of life" (14:27).

From another angle, right living makes good sense. "A kind man benefits himself" (11:17). We are told that obeying the commands of God prolongs life, brings prosperity, and wins you favor and a good name in the sight of God and humanity (3:2-4). Even a person who is not a Christian benefits from applying the commands of God to life. They are tried and true in the crucible of experience. Proverbs, then, gives us these reasons to do what is right: the command of God and good results.

Think About It

Which of Proverbs' two motivations for doing right better appeals to you? Why?

Godly Virtues

Old Testament prophets brought God's law down to a personal level. The Hebrew people often found a way to hide from individual responsibility by thinking of themselves as members of the larger covenant community. While it was true that they had a significant identity with the group, such an identity did not release them from personal responsibility for their moral choices. The days of claiming to be a victim of the sins of parents were over. As Jeremiah put it, "In those days people will no longer say, 'The fathers have eaten sour grapes, and the children's teeth are set on edge.' Instead, everyone will die for his own sin; whoever eats sour grapes—his own teeth will be set on edge" (31:29-30).

The prophets encouraged a variety of godly virtues and denounced any perversion or corruption of them. A partial list includes

- treating the poor and oppressed fairly;
- being honest in business;
- administering justice fairly in the court system;
- tending the land responsibly;
- loving God and others;
- valuing people for their intrinsic worth, not as a means to an end;
- showing compassion to the needy;
- using power and authority properly;
- using money responsibly;
- having a solid work ethic;
- worshiping God with the right spirit and attitude.

Perhaps the best summary of the ethical message of the prophets is found in Mic. 6:8: "He has showed you, O man, what is good. And what does the LORD require of you? To act justly and to love mercy and to walk humbly with your God." Justice and mercy toward others, humble fellowship with God—that's what it takes to please Him.

Think About It

If the prophets of the Old Testament were preaching today, which three of their messages does our culture most need to hear?

1.

2.

3.

Internal Source

The biggest contrast between the ethical admonitions of the Old and New Testaments comes at the point of their origins. Old Testament believers thought more in terms of external observance of external laws. The New Testament internalized all this in the human heart. The Old Testament prophets had a clear vision of this long before it came to pass. Jeremiah saw the coming internalization of God's law in 31:31-34. Verse 33 captures the essence of it: "'This is the covenant I will make with the house of Israel after that time,' declares the LORD. 'I will put my law in their minds and write it on their hearts. I will be their God, and they will be my people.'" Ezekiel expressed the same vision in his ministry with these words from God: "I will give you a new heart and put a new spirit in you; I will remove from you your heart of stone and give you a heart of flesh. And I will put my Spirit in you and move you to follow my decrees and be careful to keep my laws" (36:26-27).

We who have the privilege of living in New Testament times understand these prophecies being fulfilled in our day through the ministry of the Holy Spirit to our lives. He takes the words and deeds of Jesus Christ as recorded in the Bible and writes them deep in our hearts. The new law of the Spirit is not a legalistic observance of a dead letter, but rather a life of faith as we live in relationship with Christ himself. We are instructed and motivated to make good moral choices because God the Holy Spirit has written His law deep within us.

Think About It

Name three advantages New Testament believers have over Old Testament figures in their personal relationship with God.
1.
2.
3.

The Reality

Jeremiah and Ezekiel could say only what the Lord told them to say about the new covenant. They anticipated it, but they did not have complete understanding as to how it would be fulfilled (1 Pet. 1:10-12). Their anticipation became a reality in the life and ministry of Jesus Christ. He did not bring a different law from God, but rather a fulfillment and a model of the old Law that no one else had been able to give. He said, "Do not think that I have come to abolish the Law or the Prophets; I have not come to abolish them but to fulfill them" (Matt. 5:17). In Jesus we see God's moral principles of the Law fleshed out. He cut to the heart of God's intentions for the Law and put them into daily practice.

Jesus emphasized the moral admonitions of the Law but not the ceremonial rites and rituals. That is one of the reasons He found himself at odds with the Pharisees. He had little use for the human traditions that surrounded God's original Law. Read Mark 7:1-13 for one of Jesus' encounters with the Pharisees. Notice especially verse 9: "And he said to them: 'You have a fine way of setting aside the commands of God in order to observe your own traditions!'" Jesus knew the Father was not impressed with a strict adherence to human tradition as an end in itself. He encouraged personal and intimate fellowship with the Father as the true essence of religion. Obeying God's laws, then, springs naturally from a heart of love. Thus, God's laws are written on our hearts (through the ministry of the Holy Spirit), just as Jeremiah and Ezekiel prophesied.

In taking this stand, Jesus reminds us of an important difference between himself and the Pharisees. The Pharisees loved to create tedious laws so that their performance could be measured and judged. In fact, they had more than 600 such laws in their tradition. Jesus, on the other hand, emphasized godly principles that focused on God's original purpose rather than human laws. In so doing, He reminds us of the importance of always looking for God's intended purposes and the spirit of the Law, rather than just following a dead letter.

Think About It
1. Why do you think the Pharisees placed so much emphasis on outward performance?
2. What is the best way to discern God's intended purpose for a particular law?

In Summary
The Pharisees asked Jesus to reduce the Old Testament Law to its lowest common denominator. His reply was twofold: "Love the Lord your God with all your heart and with all your

soul and with all your mind" and "Love your neighbor as your-self" (Matt. 22:37, 39). The first command is a summary of the first four of the Ten Commandments; the second is a summary of the last six. If we love God with all we have within us, and love others as ourselves, we have met His intentions for the Law. As with the Ten Commandments, love for God comes first; love for others flows from our love for Him. On another occasion Jesus summarized the Law and the Prophets (a common reference for the Old Testament) by saying, "In everything, do to others what you would have them do to you" (7:12). We call this the Golden Rule. We must always keep the biblical principle of love for God and others at the center of our thinking as we make our moral choices.

Think About It

Why is our lo . e for God and others so crucial to living as He intends us to live?

Watch Your Attitude

Jesus picked up and strengthened the Old Testament emphasis upon guarding the internal motivation for our actions. He reminded us that the Father sees not only what we do but also what we think and feel. He looks at and judges our hearts as the fountainhead of our actions. The Old Testament said, "Do not murder"; Jesus said, "Do not have evil feelings toward others." The Old Testament said, "Do not commit adultery"; Jesus said, "Do not harbor lust in your heart." The Old Testament allowed for divorce; Jesus took it out of the discussion, except for marital unfaithfulness. The Old Testament said, "Keep your oaths"; Jesus said, "Speak so you do not need oaths." The Old Testament allowed for limited revenge; Jesus said we should not want revenge. The Old Testament said, "Love your neighbor"; Jesus said, "Love everyone—even your enemies." If we live in this manner, we can be perfect, as our Father in heaven is perfect (see Matt. 5:21-48).

Jesus placed central focus on the human heart when He said, "Don't you see that whatever enters the mouth goes into the stomach and then out of the body? But the things that come out of the mouth come from the heart, and these make a man 'unclean'" (Matt. 15:17-18). Our motivation for following God's law raises it to a whole new level of living and gives us another biblical principle for making moral choices. Be sure your heart is in your right choices.

Think About It
What will eventually happen to us if we follow God's law outwardly but our heart is not in it?

A New Creation
The apostle Paul reminds us that our ethical choices flow from an entirely different way of thinking than the world uses, because we are "a new creation; the old has gone, the new has come!" (2 Cor. 5:17). Our new creation gives us a new focus for thinking and living. The apostle says, "Set your minds on things above, not on earthly things" (Col. 3:2). In several places and in different ways Paul discusses the contrast between our old and new lives. In Col. 3 he gives the image of putting to death everything that belonged to our earthly nature. He provides quite a lengthy list of items in verses 5 through 9. In their place are the manifestations of our new creation. He then gives the virtues that characterize our lives—virtues like compassion, kindness, humility, gentleness, patience, forbearance, forgiveness, love, perfect unity, the peace of Christ, thankfulness, worship, and gratitude (vv. 12-17). Every time we are called upon to make a moral choice, we should remind ourselves that we are a new creation and see which of Paul's lists best fits our choice.

Think About It
1. Why does Paul call a believer "a new creation"?
2. What is new?

In Christ
One of Paul's favorite expressions was to remind us that we are "in Christ." By that he meant the mystical union we as believers have with the risen Lord through the ministry of the Holy Spirit. Paul was so fond of the expression that he used it more than 90 times in his Epistles. Here is a sampling of the benefits we receive from being "in Christ":
- freedom from condemnation to sin—Rom. 8:1
- sanctification and a call to be holy—1 Cor. 1:2
- the grace of God—1 Cor. 1:4
- righteousness, holiness, redemption—1 Cor. 1:30

- a way of life—1 Cor. 4:17
- hope—1 Cor. 15:19
- spiritual life—1 Cor. 15:22
- the promises of God—2 Cor. 1:20
- firm standing—2 Cor. 1:21
- removal of the veil from the old covenant—2 Cor. 3:14
- new creation—2 Cor. 5:17
- our sins not counted against us—2 Cor. 5:19
- spiritual freedom—Gal. 2:4
- justified in God's sight—Gal. 2:16
- the riches of God's grace—Eph. 2:7
- God's forgiveness—Eph. 4:32
- the peace of God—Phil. 4:7

The vital relationship we have with God in Christ is a powerful motivation for making wise *ethical* lifestyle choices.

Think About It

What privileges of being "in Christ" do you most enjoy?
1.
2.
3.

The Power of the Holy Spirit

Paul never assumed for a minute that a believer could live the Christian life and make consistently wise ethical choices by ordinary human power. Ability to do that comes only through the power of the Holy Spirit, which is given to those who abide in Christ. The Spirit justifies us in God's sight, cleanses us from all sin, and sanctifies us (1 Cor. 6:11; Rom. 15:16). He gives us gifts to be used for the edifying of the Christian community (1 Cor. 12:1-13). He gives us a whole new lifestyle through our faith in Christ. Because He lives within us, the Bible refers to our bodies as the "temple of the Holy Spirit" (6:19). This new life will take us all the way to heaven.

Study Rom. 8 for a full description of this new life that comes by the power of the Holy Spirit. Especially notice the contrast between those who live according to their sinful natures and those who live by the Spirit. "Those who live in accordance with the Spirit have their minds set on what the Spirit desires" (v. 5). They have "life and peace" (v. 6). The same power that the Father used to raise Jesus from the dead is available to assist us in victorious living: "And if the Spirit of him who raised Jesus from the dead is living in you, he who raised Christ from the dead will also give life to your mortal bodies through his Spirit, who lives in you" (v. 11). We must always remember that those who are led by God's Spirit are God's children (v. 14). Notice throughout this passage that we make a daily choice to be led by the Spirit of God. Such leadership will assist us in making wise moral choices.

Think About It

In what way is the power of the Holy Spirit a fulfillment of the prophecies of Jeremiah and Ezekiel discussed above?

The Armor of God

Another image of Paul that is helpful when considering moral choices is found in Eph. 6:10-18. Here Paul reminds us that more is going on in our world than what we can see with our eyes. Our enemy Satan has planned our defeat. These moral choices we are called upon to make are not innocent, neutral choices. Much more is involved than selecting a television program to watch, a magazine to read, a T-shirt slogan to wear, or a joke to tell. They are pieces of a bigger puzzle, strategies in a bigger battle. Our choices and spiritual struggles are part of the cosmic battle between good and evil. Every moral choice we make either helps or hinders the cause of God. Paul goes on to describe all the components of the full armor of God, which when used properly will keep us steadfast in the heat of the spiritual battle. They include the belt of truth, the breastplate of righteousness, shoes of readiness from the gospel of peace, the shield of faith, the helmet of salvation, and the sword of the Spirit. Put on the whole armor of God so that you will be prepared to fight on God's side.

Think About It

Which items in the armor of God do you use most often?

Think Good Thoughts

No doubt Paul knew the teaching of Jesus on guarding the purity of our hearts. That's why he placed so much emphasis on controlling our thought life. Our thought life sets the pattern for our attitude and spirit. We usually act on the things on which our minds dwell. It's easier to control what goes into our thinking than it is to control illegitimate desires once they have sprung to life. That's why Paul says in Phil. 4:8-9, "Finally, brothers, whatever is true, whatever is noble, whatever is right, whatever is pure, whatever is lovely, whatever is admirable—if anything is excellent or praiseworthy—think about such things. Whatever you have learned or received or heard from me, or seen in me—put it into practice. And the God of peace will be with you." We should keep these verses in mind as we consider moral choices that give us food for thought. Many sights and sounds of our culture, especially from the media, are not worth taking into our lives. We must guard the gate to our mind.

Think About It

Name two areas of your life in which you should remember Phil. 4:8-9 when making decisions.
1.
2.

Consider Others

Paul introduces an important component for us to consider as we contemplate moral decisions. It is found in 1 Cor. 10:23— 11:1, in which he discusses the matter of Christians eating meat offered to idols as an illustration of their religious freedom. Paul acknowledges that as long as believers understand that it is not a violation of their allegiance to God, it is not a problem for them to eat meat that has been consecrated to idols.

However, our freedom and conscience are not the only considerations (10:29). We must also think of the spiritual welfare of weaker believers who may not understand our freedom. We must not willfully do anything that will cause them to lose faith. We must seek not only our good "but the good of others" as well (v. 24). Paul is not saying that we must live in bondage to other people's personal convictions. That would be a hopeless situation. He is saying that we must be sensitive to the people who are watching our lives so that we do not purposefully cause them to stumble. In thinking of the bigger picture, Paul reminds us to do everything "for the glory of God" (v. 31). So when making moral decisions, don't forget to consider the beliefs of those who are watching your spiritual life.

Think About It

Think of an example from your own life in which your spiritual freedom might cause someone to stumble.

Resident Aliens

Another of Paul's images comes from Phil. 3:20: "Our citizenship is in heaven." We will discuss this concept more fully in chapter 9. At this point, think about the attitude of a traveler passing through a foreign country. He or she does not put down roots or get too attached to the local life. Paul was actively involved in taking the gospel message to his world, but he always considered himself to be an alien longing for his heavenly home. We should adopt that same mentality as we live our lives on this earth. That which we see with our natural eyes is not all there is to God's reality. We have our eyes set on a heavenly vision. That vision affects every moral lifestyle choice we make.

Think About It

Think of an inconvenience you tolerate while on vacation because you know you'll be back home soon and things will return to normal. Now transfer that concept to your spiritual life, and think of an inconvenience you can better tolerate in this life because you know you'll be going to heaven someday.

Love God and Others

The apostle John had several concepts around which he developed his ethic. Perhaps his most frequent reference was to an ethic of love, which he learned from the life and ministry of Jesus. He said everything we do should be from a heart of love for God and one another. He discussed love 21 times in his Gospel and 24 times in 1 John. He could hardly discuss any subject without bringing love into it.

Love begins with God, who loved us first: "As the Father has loved me, so have I loved you. Now remain in my love" (John 15:9). It continues with our loving one another: "By this all men will know that you are my disciples, if you love one another" (13:35). Jesus reminds us that the best way we show God that we love Him is by obeying His commands (14:15-24). Watch for the love theme as you read John's writings.

Think About It

Why do you suppose the apostle John loved Jesus so much?

Black and White

John thought of ethical choices with very clear-cut categories. Issues were never shades of gray; they were black or white. That's why so many of his discussions were presented in terms of light and darkness, life and death, righteousness and sin, and good and evil. Each of these contrasting concepts are worth your study time. They are always very sharp distinctions. John says we must choose one side or the other. For example, take the metaphor of light. God is light. Jesus brought us spiritual light; we should make decisions that will identify us as children of the light: "But whoever lives by the truth comes into the light, so that it may be seen plainly that what he has done has been done through God" (John 3:21). To do otherwise identifies us as children of darkness (v. 19).

Regardless of the metaphor John uses, the contrast is always the same. Our ethical choices are either good and righteous and made in the light and lead us closer to eternal life, or they are bad and sinful and made in darkness and lead us toward eternal death. Sometimes our popular culture offers such persuasive arguments that we are almost convinced of their merit. John reminds us to filter these arguments through God's eternal perspective and see their reality as He sees them.

Think About It

Why does culture want to represent all ethical choices as some shade of gray rather than black or white as John says?

Good Wins

In the Book of Revelation, John places our earthly choices in eternal perspective. So often when confronted with choices, we're tempted to think, "What difference does it make?" John reminds us that our choices make a great deal of difference. God allowed him to turn to the last chapter of human history on earth and see how things will ultimately end. His report back to us is a glorious one: God and good finally win. God is sovereign over His universe. Although it has seemed at times that evil was going to triumph and matters were out of hand,

God has always been in control. When the battle is over, He and those on His side will conquer all. We should therefore be encouraged and continue to fight for what is good and right.

Think About It

1. Do thoughts of heaven and final victory encourage your heart as they did John's?
2. How can you encourage someone with this hope?

In Conclusion

This ends our brief survey of a few of the themes and passages from the Bible that offer us help in making ethical decisions. Many other themes and passages are contained in God's Word that are worth careful study. The entire Book of James, for example, is written from an ethical perspective. As you have time, you will want to study James as he discusses the ethical ramifications of hearing and doing, faith and works, use and misuse of the tongue, and the rich and the poor.

Even though this survey has been brief, it has pointed out the rich resources the Bible has to offer us as we consult it for direction in making wise ethical decisions. God does not leave us on our own to work through the maze of moral possibilities. As James reminds us, "If any of you lacks wisdom, he should ask God, who gives generously to all without finding fault, and it will be given to him" (1:5). The Spirit of God is faithful to guide us with God's Word as we seek His direction. That's why the psalmist said, "Your word is a lamp to my feet and a light for my path" (119:105).

In our next three chapters we will explore practical strategies for applying these biblical principles so that we can line up our faith with our conduct.

7

Line 'em Up: Part 1

*Strategies for Lining Up
Your Personal Life with Your Faith*

Show Us How

This past summer the president of our university, Richard Spindle, called a special task force together for an all-day meeting to discuss the future of the university and ways we could better accomplish our mission. The committee was composed of school administrators, denominational district superintendents, members of the Board of Trustees, faculty members, and students. I was one of the faculty representatives. At one point in the afternoon discussion Dr. Spindle asked Kendra, a female student representative, a pointed question: "What do you as a student want from our faculty?" Kendra looked down at the table and thought for a moment. At that time my mind went into high gear, formulating possible answers to the question. I was particularly interested in her response, since it related directly to my colleagues and me. My list of possible answers included

- a top-notch education;
- guidance in learning how to be successful in my chosen profession;
- a friend;
- someone to take an interest in me outside of class.

Her answer caught me off guard. She said, "We students want the faculty to show us how to be Christians."

My first thought was, "No, that's not it—we're here to give you an education." Then almost immediately I said to myself, "Yes, that's *exactly* why we're here!" The education and the friendship should be a part of the picture, but our primary task as professors at a Christian university is to model Christianity for our students. That's the purpose of the next three chapters—practical, down-to-earth strategies for living a truly Christian life in a world that does not comprehend or value such a lifestyle. I have divided these strategies into three categories: personal life, community life, and relationship with the world. The rest of this chapter will deal with personal life. The following two chapters will discuss the remaining categories.

Each strategy is intended as a thought provoker for individuals or a discussion starter for groups. Much more needs to be said about each—that's your task. Contemplate each strategy and find ways to apply it to your life. A list of the strategies is located at the back of the book as a handy reference for later review. Use it to go back to various strategies from time to time. Most important, make these three chapters tools that can assist you as you apply all the principles of this book into daily living.

*   *   *

STRATEGIES FOR PERSONAL LIFE

Strategy 1

Begin by checking to *see that your relationship with God is where it should be.* You cannot successfully live the Christian life if you are not in vital fellowship with God. By "vital fellowship" I mean that God is as much a necessary part of your day as the air you breathe. You cannot survive long in this world without air, and you will not survive long as a Christian without the Spirit of God living within you to energize your spirit.

If your relationship is where it ought to be, great! Read on. If it needs to be established or repaired, you can bow your head right where you are and ask God to fill you and be all He wants to be in you. That's the first step to genuine Christian living. Unfortunately, too many people in the Christian community are living defeated lives because they have just enough religion to make them miserable. That is, they attend church and follow most of the guidelines of conduct, but their lives are not empowered by the Spirit of God. They're living by their own strength. They try as hard as they can and put their best effort into it; however, eventually their human strength fails, and they feel defeated. At that point they paste a smile on their face and fake it. God never intended it to be that way. Why not take inventory and be sure your relationship with God is where it ought to be? It is vital for living the Christian life. Remember Col. 1:27: "Christ in you, the hope of glory."

Try This

Relationship with God is more an act of the will than an emotional feeling. When you check your spiritual pulse by taking inventory of your feelings, you often get a faulty reading and cause unneeded frustration for your spiritual life. You may not always feel like a Christian, but that does not make you unchristian. It is better to take spiritual inventory by looking at the resolve of your will, the motivations of your actions, and your actual lifestyle choices. Ask yourself the following questions:

1. Am I surrendered to the will of God?
2. Do I want God to live in my heart and life?
3. Do my motives and actions reflect my resolve?

Ask God to help you in any areas in which you need to make corrections or improvements.

Strategy 2

Take inventory to be sure that you are approaching life with a Christian worldview. As I said earlier in the book, our worldview is the lens through which we view all of life. It is the way we interpret reality.

We receive steady doses of competing worldviews every day. We must constantly remind ourselves that we are Christians. Then we must remind ourselves to think like Christians. The following is a brief summary of five of the most important components of a Christian worldview. You should be familiar with all of these concepts by now.

1. The belief in a God—who is sovereign, who purposefully created the world and everything in it, and who actively sustains this creation on a daily basis.
   - We deny naturalism and the belief of a reality coming about by accident.

- We deny a deistic view of God that removes Him from daily sustenance of all things.
- We assert that beyond the physical reality of our world there is a spiritual or supernatural realm.

2. The belief in a moral order: defined by God, built into all creation and reality, with objective standards of right and wrong known as universal moral law, and revealed by God to humanity.
   - We deny the relativism, subjectivism, and situationism of our culture.
   - We assert that all humanity can discover this moral order through observation of the created world, reason of the human mind, feeling of the human heart, and reading of the Christian Bible.

3. Human beings are created in and bear the image of God.
   - We are connected to the animal kingdom, but we have an added component that makes us spiritual, moral, relational, and creative.
   - All of God's creation is of worth and value, but we are qualitatively different and have a qualitatively different worth.
   - This image has been marred, but not destroyed, by sin.

4. Human beings were created good but are now corrupted by sin, both original and personal.
   - Original sin is more than flawed societal systems or a fund of bad examples from the lives of others. It is an innate predisposition of the human will found in the heart of every human being born into the world.
   - This bent toward sin leads to pride, greed, brokenness, estrangement, and a host of other paths that lead us away from God, others, and ourselves.
   - We have a very pessimistic view of the human condition, damaged by sin.

5. We believe Jesus Christ is the Second Person of the Trinity. Through His life, death, and resurrection, He broke the power of sin; He now empowers us to live our lives in conformity with His moral order.
   - We have a very optimistic view of the power of God's grace in our lives.
   - Christianity is a religion of hope and radical change.
   - We believe "the Way" of Jesus Christ is superior to all other world religions.

- We deny all attempts to lower Jesus Christ to the status of a mere man or raise our humanity to the status of deity.[1]

Try This

Ask yourself the following questions:
1. Am I thinking like a Christian?
2. What changes do I need to make for my worldview to be more Christian?

Strategy 3

Hear all that God has to say. We are so consumer oriented in this society that it becomes easy to apply a selective mind-set to our religious beliefs. The religious smorgasbord described in chapter 5 is the result of allowing culture to dictate our appetite toward God's truth. In effect, this dismantles God's perspective and serves up a piecemeal assortment of our personal preferences. Most people would prefer to create their own tailor-made religion rather than take the one God gives us.[2] We must constantly resist that common temptation.

Remember that only 13 percent of the people surveyed in *The Day America Told the Truth* believe in all of the Ten Commandments. People want to pick and choose their favorite 5 out of 10, but not all 10! I'm reminded of this tendency when some of my friends refer to God's rules as "guidelines." Do you see what we do when we downgrade a rule to a guideline? It becomes a suggestion or an option. We cannot afford this error when it comes to God and His will and plan for our lives. We must hear the *whole* message of God.

Try This

1. Answer the following questions:
   a. What Christian doctrines do you have difficulty accepting?
   b. If you had the ability, what would you like to change about the Christian message?
2. Ask God to help you in these areas of belief. Talk through your difficulties with your pastor or a trusted Christian friend.

Strategy 4

Focus your eyes to see the spiritual reality of life. Reality comes to us in three interlocking sets of environments: the physical-biological environment, the social-cultural environment, and the cosmological-spiritual environment. We live and process data in all three realms of reality all the time, usually without distinguishing between them. The physical-biological is the world around us; it is what our senses perceive. The social-cultural is the world in which we associate and interact with others. The cosmological-spiritual environment is the world in which we discuss where we came from and where we are going. It looks for answers to the spiritual questions of life. It is where we talk about truth and falsehood, beauty and ugliness, goodness and evil. We learn about God, Satan, sin, and salvation.[3]

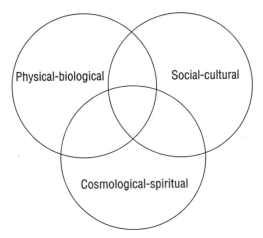

We need to remind ourselves from time to time that our ethical lifestyle choices impact us at all three levels. Take, for instance, the act of checking out a videotape to watch with friends. The videotape itself is a physical object that produces sights and sounds and contains plots and subplots, actors and scenery—all components of the physical-biological realm. The fact that you watch it with your friends sets up a social dimension. You interact as you comment on the plot or actors, as you talk about what you like and don't like, and as you share popcorn together—all components of the social-cultural realm. The videotape is filled with ideas, philosophies, and a worldview. The dialogue, the development of the plot, the use of language or violence or sex, and the outcome of the entire movie all speak to the cosmological-spiritual realm. God and godly values are either honored, ignored, or despised.

We must give careful attention to what is happening to us, our friends, our convictions, and our values with every lifestyle choice we make. More is taking place than we can see or feel. We are actually involved in the cosmic battle between good and evil. The enemy is always seeking to lead us astray. Therefore, it is our responsibility as believers to watch for sources of temptation and not surrender to our foe. Remember Eph. 6:12: "For our struggle is not against flesh and blood, but against the rulers, against the authorities, against the powers of this dark world and against the spiritual forces of evil in the heavenly realms." When we are tempted to compromise our convictions in the entertainments we choose, the places we go, the language we use, and the attitudes we adopt, we are warring against the spiritual forces of evil. As Christians, we must never forget our relationship with the spiritual realm of life.

Try This

Take a minute at the end of each day to reflect on the events of that particular day. Answer the following questions:
1. What were the cosmological or spiritual dimensions of my life today?
2. Where were the lines between good and evil?
3. What choices did I make in favor of the good?
4. What choices did I make in favor of the evil?
5. What strategies did Satan use to try to trip me up?
6. How can I strengthen my position to do even better next time?

Strategy 5

Saturate your life with the Word of God. Make it as much a part of your thinking as you can. Our world is sending us messages on the spiritual level of life throughout the day. Most of these messages do not reverence God, encourage virtue, or warn of consequences. We must counteract these false messages with the truth of God. Living in God's Word keeps us sensitive to His values and helps us see life from the divine perspective.

Jesus is our Model. It is obvious that He kept the words of Scripture central in His thinking, as evidenced by His frequent references to it. Take, for example, the time He was led into the desert to be tempted by the devil. Each of the three times Satan offered Him something to get Him to depart from the Father's will, He countered with memorized scriptures (Matt. 4:1-11). Living in the Word will go a long way in sparing us from poor judgment and sin. As King David put it, "I have hidden your word in my heart that I might not sin against you" (Ps. 119:11).

Try This

1. Make it a priority to read your Bible daily. It will not be easy. Satan will see to it that your schedule is always filled with good and meaningful appointments or responsibilities that will keep you from God's Word. Set your daily appointment with God, and keep it.
2. Write each day on note cards meaningful Bible verses you read. Carry them with you throughout your day. Place them where your sight will catch them often. Review them throughout the day. Make them a part of your life.
3. Memorize scripture. Start with a verse at a time. You will find that the verses on your note cards get into your memory as you read them several times a day.
4. Focus on one particular verse at the end of each day. Repeat it until you can recite it from memory. The Holy Spirit will bring these verses back to you in times of need.

Strategy 6

Break down the wall in your thinking between the secular and the sacred. In other words, fight the cultural tendency to compartmentalize your life. Let your religious faith inform and pass judgment upon everything you think, say, and do in your daily life. The Hebrew people of biblical times did this. Their language did not have words that defined separate realms for secular and sacred. All of life was lived in God's sight, so all of life for them we would describe as sacred.

Viewing all of life as sacred does not mean that you act serious and straight-faced all the time. Unfortunately, some Christians, both in the past and present, have taken that view. They give Christianity a bad name. They go through life with a stiff face and one rule of conduct: If it's fun, it's sin. God never intended us to live that way. Jesus participated in joyous occasions and had lighthearted moments with His disciples.

The danger we must guard against is living a "Dr. Jekyll and Mr. Hyde" existence. That is, we must not talk and act like

Christians when we're at church or socializing with our Christian friends and then make unchristian lifestyle choices when we're by ourselves or with unchristian friends. This strategy is crucial for people of all ages. I have observed in working with generation X that the No. 1 reason they become disillusioned with Christ and His Church is because they see their parents speak and act one way at church and another way at home. Baby boomers often have the same response as they see a double lifestyle in Christian friends or people they admire in the church. The language, the attitude, the spirit, the entertainment choices, the habits, the moods all testify to something very different from their public image.

Live all of life in the sacred realm.

Try This

1. Make a conscious effort to monitor every word, action, reaction, attitude, habit, mood, and lifestyle choice you have for the next week. Ask the Holy Spirit to help you do this.
2. Note which ones are consistent with your Christian commitment.
3. Note which ones are a bit questionable with regard to your Christian commitment.
4. Note which ones are off-limits for you as a Christian.
5. Take action to bring each choice that is a bit questionable and off-limits into consistency with your Christian commitment.
6. Develop a habit of doing this exercise on an ongoing basis throughout the day.

Strategy 7

Take inventory of your personal convictions on ethical issues; know where you stand, based on the Bible and good reason, and refuse to compromise. Society constantly reminds us of the need for tolerance, and to a degree this is valid. Christians should be tolerant of the positions of others at the social level. That is, we must grant other people the space to hold views different from our own. We do not help the cause of Christ by displaying an intolerant spirit that shouts the other person down or resorts to violence. The cause of Christ is never advanced by a hateful spirit or action. However, showing tolerance is entirely different from pluralism, which contends that all these views are as equally correct as mine. They may be wrong when judged by the objective truth of God, but we extend civil courtesy to others who hold such views.

However, we must be certain of our ethical positions. Such certainty can be increased by providing additional arguments to support our beliefs. Sources for additional arguments can be our pastor, local congregation or age-group, or trusted Christian friends. Together with these supports, we can brainstorm to clarify all the reasons we hold each of our ethical positions. It is a good idea to write down these reasons and then commit them to memory. They will be helpful when you discuss your stand with non-Christian friends.

Knowing where you stand on ethical issues will prevent you from drifting aimlessly on the sea of cultural relativism, subjectivism, and pluralism. In the long run, your stand will have a greater impact than you realize. You may not know who they are, but people in your sphere of influence admire a person who takes a stand and holds true to personal convictions. You can impact them for good. Biblical convictions have a further benefit in that they build character to make you morally strong. This is because they are rooted in the nature of God, who is the Source of all true reality. So take your stand.

Try This

What is your personal conviction on five of the following ethical issues that relate to your life at this time? On a piece of paper, write your position and at least two reasons you believe this way. Think how you would defend your position in a discussion with someone.

1. Prejudice against people of other races or ethnic origins
2. Abortion when the life of the mother is not in danger
3. Pornography
4. Suicide
5. Premarital sex
6. Extramarital affairs
7. Homosexual practices
8. Social drinking
9. Secular music
10. Cursing and foul language in the media
11. Violence in the media
12. Sexually explicit or implicit material in the media
13. Lotteries, horse racing, casinos, or riverboat gambling

14. Cheating on an exam or income taxes
15. Divorce for any reason other than adultery, desertion, or an unchristian mate wanting out of the relationship
16. Disrespect for ministers and religion in society and the media
17. Loose talk about sex
18. Defining your worth by material possessions
19. Using all your time and money for your personal interests
20. Off-color jokes

Strategy 8

Carefully guard what you allow your mind to dwell upon. Don't think about it unless you're prepared to act upon it, because chances are good that given enough time, you probably will. Thoughts come to us from two basic sources: from within and from without. Thoughts originating from within have their source in our hearts, the seat of our desires, intentions, and will. We value something enough that we entertain thoughts about it. Thoughts originating from without come to us from our environment: television, radio, magazines, billboards. Satan can use any of these channels to present us with material upon which to center our thinking. If he can get us to entertain thoughts in a certain area, he can break down our resistance and make us susceptible to sin. Counselors are wrong when they tell us that mental fantasy is a harmless form of personal entertainment. It can be deadly.

This past week I heard a Christian baby boomer tell how she fell into the sin of adultery. She said it all began with an innocent touch on her hand from a married man. She lingered just long enough to entertain thoughts of affection. She said her Christian reason warned her to put it out of her mind quickly, but she harbored the thoughts long enough for them to germinate into a desire. The desire would not weaken, so she yielded to sin and had an affair.

No doubt Eve's failure in the Garden of Eden began long before she bit into the forbidden fruit. Her problems started when she wore a path around the tree of the knowledge of good and evil and began to dwell on thoughts about the luscious taste of the forbidden fruit. Moral failure followed closely upon the heels of her fantasy. So carefully guard your thought life.

Try This

1. For the next week, monitor your thought life carefully.
2. See if you can distinguish the source of your thoughts from within or from without.
3. Are the thoughts coming from your heart consistent with your Christian commitment?
4. Are the thoughts coming from your environment consistent with your Christian commitment?
5. Do they bring temptations with them?
6. Ask God to help you develop the skill of rejecting all thoughts inconsistent with your Christian commitment. Like building muscles, you will become stronger with practice.

Strategy 9

Control the flow. Our society is addicted to entertainment at every age level. We have music or television playing almost every waking hour of every day. It has a powerful influence on our thinking processes as well as our lifestyle choices.

We should not judge all music and television programming as negative. Not all of it is. From it we learn many good things about life and the experiences of others, about feelings and emotions, about tragedy and triumph. The media makes us laugh and cry. It puts us in touch with ourselves and our world. Entertainment comes in a variety of styles for everyone's varying tastes.

The danger we must guard against is addiction. One of life's simple pleasures for me is an occasional Twinkie, but I don't eat a plate of Twinkies three times a day. That would be an addiction! Our problem is in never turning off the radio or television or stereo or Walkman. Most of my friends don't look at a television guide to see if anything is worth watching. They mindlessly turn on the television set and watch whatever is being dished up at that time. The addiction can become so complete that we can't stand to be separated from our entertainment. We must have something playing every waking hour.

Here's an interesting illustration of this point. I do my clearest thinking when I am in nature, so I've been thinking about this material while sitting in the woods. A man just walked by me taking a hike through the woods. As he went by, I noticed he was watching a palm-sized television set. He apparently could not be disconnected from media long enough to take a nature hike. That's addiction! If we remain addicted long enough, we lose touch with reality and the true nature of things and adopt the false reality of the entertainment world.

Television is the single most shared experience in our entire society. It now has a role once reserved for God: the role of defining reality.[4] In the world of television, all of life's problems can be solved in 30 to 120 minutes. Sex, money, and power rule. Choices have no lasting consequences. Grooming products and soft drinks can make our lives meaningful. We should think only of our needs in the here and now. The net results are impatience, boredom, and short attention spans. The media gives us the novel and promises instant gratification. But it promises more than it can deliver. So we're never satisfied and are constantly in search of something more. If it can't give an answer to life's deepest questions, at least it can numb the pain for one more day. This sounds very strange when you analyze it from the outside, but if you're in the media cycle, it makes perfect sense. You are oblivious to anything else.[5]

That is where we Christians must be different from our non-Christian friends. We must break the addiction, step outside the cycle, see what is happening to us, and keep a firm grip on the true reality of God and our relationship with Him. I don't feel God expects us to divorce ourselves completely from media, even if it were possible; I do believe He expects us to control it so that it doesn't control us.

Try This

1. Make a chart on which you record your television viewing for a week. List the following information:
   Day of the week Turn-on time Turn-off time Programs watched
   Note whether you planned to watch each program or watched it simply because it was on at the time.
2. At the end of the week, tally up how many hours you watched television each day, and total them for the week.
3. See how much you watched television just to have it on.

4. Decide if you are watching more television than is best for you. Set a plan to cut back if necessary and select activities to replace it.
5. Do this same exercise with your radio.

Strategy 10

Analyze the return on your investment. This strategy follows from the last one. The reason people get so addicted to the media is because of diminishing returns. You know the principle well: a drug addict must take larger and larger doses to get the same high. A pornography addict must view more and more perverse materials to feel satisfied. A gambling addict must play longer hours and at higher stakes to get the same rush.

The same is true with media. Consider the television and movie industries. We want to see bigger-and-bigger-budget productions with more dramatic special effects. A movie producer who was interviewed regarding his third installment of a film series said it was hard to produce because, as he put it, "What do you do when you've done it all?" The same is true with music videos. Each new video needs an edge—something to separate it from the rest of the pack and cause us consumers to prefer it. So music videos present us with an infinite variety of sights and sounds to intrigue our imagination.

Nothing in media can satisfy the deepest need of the human heart. We can up the dosage as often as we want, but the result is the same—dissatisfaction. Remember: media itself is not as much the problem as our false hope that it will fulfill us. As a temporary diversion from the stresses of life or as a source of information, it works fine. As an answer for ultimate fulfillment, we get only diminishing returns.

Try This

1. Think of two areas in your experience that illustrate the principle of diminishing returns.
   a.
   b.
2. The only way to stop the cycle is to cease the practice or action. Write out a plan to break the cycle of diminishing returns in your life.
3. Think of two ways to keep yourself from falling into this trap again.

a.

b.

Strategy 11

Look past the surface messages of media to the deeper agenda being presented. The various negative themes and components of television and the movies have been extensively explored in other works.[6] We are all familiar with the levels of violence, sex, crude language, depreciation of family values, and lack of respect for God, religious faith, and religious people. We are also familiar with the negative themes in popular music: drug and alcohol usage, marital unfaithfulness, sexual promiscuity and perversion, violence, disrespect for parents and other authority figures, Satan worship, and all-out rebellion against the establishment.

But what about the deeper, philosophical agendas coming to us through the media? They are far more subtle and perhaps more dangerous than the obvious. Our mental guard goes up when we see or hear the obvious offenses; the subtle tends to sneak by us unobserved. That's what makes it so dangerous— these worldly philosophies enter our mind and work on our thinking processes without our awareness of what is happening. That's why media must be viewed at two levels: the surface message and the underlying philosophy. Again, not everything in the media is bad, but we must be careful.

Here is a partial list of some of the dangers of the media:

1. It offers a false view of reality. It teaches that
   a. truth is relative;
   b. true meaning in life comes through materialism;
   c. immediate personal gratification is our birthright.
2. It offers us celebrities who are not heroes.
   a. A celebrity is a person with face or name recognition.
   b. A hero is a person of virtue and honor who lives by ethical principles.
3. It can destroy self-esteem and self-worth.
   a. Physical beauty is presented as a requirement for personal worth.
   b. Ownership of material possessions is required for a person to be somebody.
4. It makes real life boring.
   a. What in the real world can possibly compete with the spe-

cial effects, the fast-moving camera angles, or the quick scene changes?

b. Our attention spans and interests become short and narrowly focused.

5. It presents unchristian images of Christians.

a. No award night in Hollywood is complete without godless actors and actresses thanking God for their success and leading us to believe they are Christians.

b. Television programs present ministers and even angels taking God's name in vain and displaying evil attitudes or actions or both.

c. Rock music often incorporates religious language and themes in its lyrics with a very unholy message.[7]

Try This

Walt Mueller offers the following list of questions to ask of the media. Make it a habit to ask these questions about the television program you are watching or the music you are hearing.

1. What does it say about God?
2. What does it say about humanity?
3. Is the one true God replaced by some other deity (self, money, and so on)?
4. What does it say about happiness?
5. Is it hopeful or hopeless?
6. What does it say about the nature of sexuality?
7. Are solutions offered to life's problems? What are they?
8. Who is the hero?
9. Who is the villain?
10. What character traits are promoted as positive? negative?
11. How is beauty and personal worth established and defined?
12. How is the family portrayed?[8]

Strategy 12

Consider the consequences. Regardless of what our society tells us, our actions, reactions, attitudes, and motives have consequences. Some of them are good, others bad. Some of them are temporary; others last for a lifetime or an eternity. Some of them affect only the person involved; others spill over into the lives of innocent friends and family members.

Allan Bloom notes, "Choice is all the rage these days, but it does not mean what it used to mean." When people speak of the right choice these days, they mean there are no necessary consequences. Disapproval is only prejudice, and guilt only a neurosis. America has no-fault auto accidents and no-fault divorces, and it is moving toward no-fault choices.[9] When the consequences are negative, we try to find some person or organization to blame. We are the victim. Victimization is the new national craze. This phenomenon is documented in Charles Sykes's book *A Nation of Victims: The Decay of the American Character.* If you work your case properly through the court system, you may even be fortunate enough to be awarded a large sum of money for your unwise choice!

We have a commitment as Christians to take responsibility for our actions. We don't blame others; we don't try victimization. Everyone has had negative experiences that could leave us bitter and blaming others if we chose to take that route; we do not. An important feature of our Christian responsibility is the foresight to count the cost of our choices before we make them. This deals not only with issues of morality but also with issues of prudence and good judgment. Constantly remind yourself that your actions always have consequences.

Try This

1. Think through the possible negative consequences on yourself and others for the following actions:
   a. Lying to a coworker, family member, friend, or authority figure
   b. Cheating on a business deal
   c. Stealing from a retail store
   d. Gambling
   e. Social drinking
   f. Viewing pornography
   g. Possessing illegal drugs
2. Think through the possible positive consequences on yourself and others for the following actions:
   a. Telling the truth in a difficult situation
   b. Being honest in a tough business deal, even if it costs you money
   c. Going the extra mile in helping an acquaintance who you feel may not deserve it
   d. Sharing with someone in need at work or school
   e. Turning off a videotape you're watching with family or

friends because the material violates your personal convictions

   f. Refusing to participate in an action because it would hurt someone's feelings
3. Develop a habit of stopping to count the possible consequences, both positive and negative, on you and the ones you love for every moral choice you make.

Strategy 13

Train your conscience. I know you expected me to say, "Let your conscience be your guide." But conscience can be flawed. It is a unique feature of humanity, placed in us by God to guide us in making good choices. But it is only as effective as the information that has been programmed into it.

Let me illustrate. I purchased a new computer for my office last year. It represented the latest technology available. But when I unpacked it, it could not perform a single function except to beep at me every time I tried to get it to do something. Each beep represented a little voice in the computer that said, "You don't know what you're doing." I may be paranoid, but I think it was also laughing at me! I was so frustrated. I spent the entire first day loading information into the hard drive. First came the operating system, then the word processing program, then the database program, then the spreadsheet program, then the desktop publishing program, and finally the screen savers. Only after all of that information was loaded into the computer could I type a letter or figure grades or make a poster. The computer was only as good as the software that made it function.

The same is true with our conscience. It works only as effectively as it has been trained and heeded. We can short-circuit our conscience in several ways:

- by failing to load information regarding right and wrong into it
- by loading incorrect information into it
- by denying its authority
- by ignoring its warnings until we no longer hear them

We see many examples of these in our society today. Many children are not taught right from wrong by their parents or guardians; it is one of the leading causes of moral anarchy in our land. Other people are misinformed and load information contrary to God's Word that grants permission to violate His objective standard of right and wrong. Even if our conscience has received proper training, we can disregard it as old-fashioned, outdated advice. We can also occupy ourselves to the point that we don't hear its warnings. We then become calloused so that we no longer hear warnings. So make sure your conscience has been informed by God's Word; then listen to it along with a variety of other spiritual sources.

Try This

Increase your understanding of conscience by answering the following questions:

1. List three sources that have informed your conscience.
   a.
   b.
   c.
2. What happens in your heart and mind when you violate your conscience?
3. What happens to your thinking when you continuously disregard your conscience at a particular point?

Think of three ways to help you remain sensitive to your conscience.

1.
2.
3.

Strategy 14

Keep temptation in perspective. The fact that we are tempted does not mean we are spiritually weak or must yield. Too many of my friends misunderstand temptation in one or both of these ways. Jesus Christ was tempted, yet He lived closer to the Father than anyone else who ever lived on this earth. As long as we are on earthly probation, we will be temptable.

The only thing Satan or our worldly environment can do is offer suggestions to us. Always remember—they can only suggest. They cannot force our free will into making us yield. That is why it is incorrect to offer the excuse "The devil made me do it." The devil cannot make us do anything. It sounds so simple, but never forget it—we do not have to yield to temptation. Our victory over temptation comes with these steps:

- Counter temptation's attack with Scripture, as Jesus did (Matt. 4:1-11).

- Flee quickly, as Joseph fled from the home of Potiphar (Gen. 39:12).
- Continue to resist when the thoughts attempt to return (James 4:7).
- Trust in God's faithfulness to help you be victorious (1 Cor. 10:13)

Try This

1. How does Satan attempt to break down your resistance to get you to yield to temptation?
2. What suggestions does Satan offer you to counter your better judgment?
3. What are Satan's best weapons against you?
4. Commit to memory the steps to keeping victory over temptation. Use them the next time Satan tempts you.

Strategy 15

Remember in your ethical decision-making that you are preparing your soul for eternity. Eternal life begins when we accept Christ as our personal Savior. Christ rules in our hearts, which affects the way we live. Even though we are still living our lives on this earth, the hope of heaven dominates our thinking. Our ethical choices are made on the basis of our heavenly reasoning. You have probably heard someone call this life "a training ground for heaven," and it is. We develop our allegiance for God and godly things here. But it is more. In a very real sense, we set our desires and affections for heaven in this life. Chief among our desires is the desire to know and love God and seek to do those things that are pleasing in His sight (Rom. 12:2).

The writer of the Book of Hebrews illustrated this point with reference to the life of Moses. Moses had experienced the privileged lifestyle of Pharaoh's palace. He could have continued to enjoy the rest of his days on this earth in luxury if he so chose, but he did not. He chose, rather, to identify himself with the Hebrew people, God's people, "than to enjoy the pleasures of sin for a short time" (11:24-25). The same choice is ours. We can indulge in the sinful pleasures of this life, or we can identify with God's people and train ourselves for heaven.

We must guard our affections carefully while we live on this earth. As John reminds, "Do not love the world or anything

in the world" (1 John 2:15). He does not mean we are not to enjoy nature. God placed beautiful scenery here for our enjoy-
ment. He loves it when we have an inspired moment enjoying
the beauty of His world. Rather, John means that we must not
fall in love with the world's sinful choices. Our souls are heav-
en-bound, and that makes a difference in our lifestyle. We have
left the world behind in pursuit of a higher goal than just meeting material needs or enjoying ourselves. Every activity in life
should be measured according to the way it affects our commitment to Christ.

Try This

Think through some of the ethical choices you have made in the
past week. Answer the following questions about them.
1. Did you make the choice quickly or with reasoned thought?
2. Did you think about the spiritual implications of the choice?
3. Did your choice line up with your faith and reflect your commitment to Christ?
4. Did your choice help prepare you for heaven, or did it take
   your affections in a direction away from heaven?
Think through these questions as you make future ethical choices.

This concludes the strategies for lining up your personal
lives with your faith. Obviously this is not an exhaustive list;
space does not allow us to say everything that ought to be said.
Hopefully these ideas will spark your thinking into other strategies you can use to improve your personal life.

The following are guides I give my students. They offer
practical questions you can ask yourself and steps you can take
to work through the process of making wise ethical decisions. I
have found them very helpful; I hope you will as well.

GUIDELINES FOR MAKING
ETHICAL DECISIONS

In making an ethical decision about a particular action, ask
yourself the following questions.
1. Will this hurt my physical well-being in any way (have a
   detrimental effect on my body, tear it down, make it less effective, make it more susceptible to disease, or harm vital
   organs)?

2. Will this hurt my mental well-being (cripple, dwarf, befog, or drag my mind to a low level)?
3. Will this hurt my spiritual well-being (hinder my spiritual life, dim my consciousness of God, cloud my Christian experience, or take the keen edge off spiritual things)?
4. What is the influence of this act upon society? (Would I want everyone else in society to do this?)
   a. Do I want to give my Christian vote in favor of this influence?
   b. Do I want to give my money, which God has made me steward over, to maintain and perpetuate this?
   c. Do I want to give my energy and time to this?
5. What will my participation in this action do to my witness as a Christian and my personal impact on the good of the community?
6. Even if I don't see anything wrong with this action, will I hurt others if they see me participating in it?
7. Does this action have any relationship to known evil?
   a. Is the atmosphere wholesome and conducive for a Christian?
   b. Does it have any appearance of evil about it?
   c. What is the character of the people associated with it?
   d. What are the implications and involvements in the future?
8. Does it contribute to the balanced Christian life for a whole person—physically, mentally, socially, and spiritually?
9. Does it have a spirit of worldliness about it (a spirit of indulgence, greed, self-interest, resentment, retaliation, vainglory, domination, or self-pity)?
10. What would Jesus do or have me do in this situation?

John Wesley's mother reminds us, "Whatever weakens your reason, impairs the tenderness of your conscience, obscures your sense of God, or takes off the relish of spiritual things, whatever increases the authority of your body over mind, that thing for you is sin."[10]

STEPS TO MAKING AN ETHICAL DECISION

1. Consult the Bible for directives. (Most questions can be answered here.)
2. Seek the guidance of the Holy Spirit; specifically request His help with your question.

3. Analyze and research the issue.
   a. Gather information.
   b. Try to understand the problem as clearly as possible.
   c. Distinguish between facts, opinions, and interpretations.
4. Seek to be as objective as possible.
   a. Remember that, given enough time, we can rationalize almost anything.
   b. Compare your reasoning with the will of God.
5. Identify, interpret, and apply biblical principles on related issues.
6. Examine your motives.
   a. What is the real reason I am questioning this?
   b. Why do/don't I want to do this?
7. What goal do you have in mind when a decision is reached?
8. Draw upon the spiritual resources of Christian friends.
9. Once a decision is reached, conduct an adequate evaluation.
   a. Did I honestly seek to do the right thing?
   b. Was I true to my conscience?
   c. Did I openly seek to find and do God's will?
   d. Am I trying to rationalize what I want to do?
10. Rely on God's strength to make good moral choices.[11]

8

Line 'em Up: Part 2

Strategies for Lining Up Your Community Life with Your Faith

Strategy 16

See your individualism in the context of the larger Christian community. Frenchman Alexis de Tocqueville came to the United States in the 1830s to study our nation. He reported his findings in the book *Democracy in America.* He called our mores "habits of the heart." These are notions, opinions, and ideas that "shape mental habits," "the sum of moral and intellectual dispositions of men in society."[1] Tocqueville said one of the most influential habits of the heart shaping America was individualism. He defined it as "a calm and considered feeling which disposes each citizen to isolate himself from the mass of his fellows and withdraw into the circle of family and friends; with this little society formed to his taste, he gladly leaves the greater society to look after itself."[2] What Tocqueville said of Americans 165 years ago remains true today: we love our individualism.

Tocqueville said individualism would work as a philosophy of life in America only as long as the nation gave an important place to religion for reinforcing self-control and maintaining moral standards. He warned that if we dislocated ourselves from a solid foundation in Christianity, our individualism would drive us into a thousand different directions and lead to moral anarchy.[3] His prophecy has been fulfilled in our day. The only individualism that really works is one that remains tied to the larger community and tradition. Total individualism leaves us personally empty and lost, a life without connection and relatedness.[4]

American Christians love their individualism as much as any other citizens of this nation. It is a part of our national identity. Baby boomer lifestyles are a personification of individualism. My generation X students express this same sentiment often in class. They view as a birthright their individual right to make personal choices without the influence of any other individual or group. However, we must recapture our self-image in the context of the Christian community of which we are members. Membership is always voluntary, never mandatory. This reminds us that we have used our individualism to commit ourselves to the larger community in much the same way we commit ourselves to a mate or other family member. Such a commitment to the Christian community is vital to our spiritual well-being.

We must also remember that we bond together for the common good of the group. The Body of Christ consists of more than a group of autonomous individuals who come together for weekly worship. Individuals who commit themselves to this Body become an organism through the power of the Spirit of God, who works within us. Membership in the Body must have a vital impact on our lifestyle choices. We often make many of our lifestyle choices on the basis of individual or personal reasoning more than on the standards of the larger community. This is not wise. We find from the Body of Christ much-needed strength for living our Christian lives. We dare not separate ourselves from it in individual isolation.

Try This

Examine some of your more recent lifestyle choices. Evaluate how much the following factors contributed to each choice.
1. Church congregation
2. The Bible
3. Family members
4. Peers
5. Social standards
6. Personal preference

Strategy 17

Remember that as a member of the Christian community, you are not alone. One of the chief complaints of both baby boomers and generation X is a constant feeling of aloneness. Boomers have divorced in record numbers, leaving generation X to suffer the ravaging effects more than any in recent history. The divorce rate among baby boomers doubled in one generation. One in four children is now born without a father in the home.[5] Generation Xers are the latchkey kids who came home from school to an empty house every afternoon. They are the kids who saw their fathers two weekends a month. They are the young adults who are afraid of the same failures, so they postpone marriage until later in life.

This sense of loneliness was the motivation for William Mahedy and Janet Bernardi writing *A Generation Alone*. They predict that we'll see this generation bond themselves together to form family-like units more than any previous generation in our nation's history. They remind us that the Christian community already offers such a family-like social unit. It is a safe haven to any who feel like strangers in their own society. Those without a strong sense of family bonding, those who feel alienated, those who feel abandoned are not lost. God is looking for all of us in the depths of our aloneness. He brings us together to form a new family—His family. That's why the Christian community is called "the family of God." It's a family with no strangers and no reason for anyone to feel alone. We have a refuge in one another and in Him.

Try This

1. Think of three ways the Christian community is like a family.
   a.
   b.
   c.
2. Think of two reasons why Christians should never feel alone. (For a start, read Matt. 18:20; 28:20; Gen. 28:15; Exod. 33:14; Isa. 43:2.)
   a.
   b.

Strategy 18

Make yourself accountable to the Christian community. Accountability is not a popular concept in our society. We hear the message of personal autonomy and rights on a daily basis; little is said of answering to others for one's life. Yet that is exactly what we need to do. Accountability was a central feature of the successful ministry of John Wesley in the 18th century. His class meetings and cell groups brought people together in nurturing relationships. Those of us in the Wesleyan tradition have a rich heritage of accountability. The Bible urges us to get together as a body of believers not only for corporate worship but also to look out for one another. That is the thinking behind the admonition in Gal. 6:2: "Carry each other's burdens, and in this way you will fulfill the law of Christ." We make ourselves responsible to one another.

This is exactly the opposite of what personal autonomy encourages. As Robert Bellah puts it, "If the individual self must be its own source of moral guidance, then each individual must always know what he wants and desires or intuit what he feels. He must act so as to produce the greatest satisfaction of his wants or to express the fullest range of his impulses."[6] We don't always know what is best for us, and we certainly don't know what may be best in the long run of life. We simply don't have enough information or perfect reasoning skills with which to decide. Instead of a call from the group to follow God's will, personal autonomy has the subjective pull to get and enjoy what it wants.

Christianity, with its accountability, operates from a different perspective. It is a commitment to the obedience of God's Word. It is based less on feeling and more on decision and action. Obligation takes precedence over feelings.[7] We hold each other in the Body of Christ responsible for that. Christians encourage one another toward faithfulness to God and His standards for our lives.

The research of Patterson and Kim shows that people who are accountable to others make far better citizens. They obey the law and are more moral than those who live to themselves and keep their secrets. When people are open to accountability, they are transparent, because what is inside them is good. On the other hand, those who keep their secrets tend to be less satisfied with themselves, have more violent impulses, and act more on those impulses.[8]

So make yourself accountable to the Christian community.

Try This

1. Find yourself a Christian accountability partner: someone with whom you can confide who will keep your relationship in confidence.

2. Share with him or her on a weekly basis regarding your spiritual life and lifestyle choices.
3. Give this person permission to ask you anything about your spiritual life and lifestyle choices.
4. Admit to this person your areas of weakness and temptation.
5. Pray together and encourage each other in the faith.

Strategy 19

Maintain your connection to community tradition. Tradition is defined in the dictionary as the ways in which we pass our culture down from one generation to the next. It represents the time-honored beliefs and practices of society. Our society once honored tradition. No more. It no longer has a sense of community with respect for the ways our ancestors believed and lived. Civil community tradition has always played an important role in establishing and maintaining good ethical standards. It is one of the foundations of moral responsibility. One of the chief downfalls of a pluralistic society is the depreciation of community bonding and tradition. Such a society cuts itself loose from its own past. In eliminating these important features of our society, we create an autonomous self-existence that operates independent of tradition.[9]

Our need for community tradition can still be met, however, even in the absence of respect for civil tradition. As members of the Christian community, we find not only accountability to one another but also a connection to the past through the lives of older and departed saints and a source of moral strength to follow in their footsteps. Stanley Hauerwas and William Willimon make an important statement about Christian tradition when they say, "Tradition . . . is a complex, lively argument about what happened in Jesus that has been carried on, across the generations, by a concrete body of people called the church. Fidelity to this tradition, this story, is the most invigorating challenge of the adventure begun in our baptism and the toughest job of Christian ethics."[10]

We learn good moral principles by looking at the example of other believers in the Christian community. Christian ethics, as a discipline, is simply the task of assembling reminders that enable us to remember how we should speak and live the language of the gospel as it has been passed down to us through church history.[11] This not only keeps us in touch with our past but also gives us guidance for our daily choices.

Try This

Reflect on answers to these questions:
1. Why is it important to stay in touch with your past?
2. What benefits do traditions offer in helping us make good moral decisions?
3. What do you think motivates some adopted children to seek out their biological parents when they reach adulthood?
4. What does this say about our need as Christians to remain connected to our religious heritage?

Strategy 20

Submit yourself to the corporate conscience of the Christian community. This strategy is a logical conclusion of the last two strategies. Corporate conscience is a very sound principle. Many Christians who have gone before us on the journey of life have learned some valuable lessons, both good and bad. Their decisions create a fund of advice. This advice comes from many voices over a long period of time. We can benefit from their experiences. The individualism of our day urges us to be responsible to no one. Common sense advises otherwise.

Baby boomers and generation Xers have especially had a problem with the concept of corporate conscience. Partly because of the social rebellion of the 1960s and partly because of the cry for personal autonomy, we want to go our own way. If we aren't careful, this spirit of the age can create a spiritual problem. We can reject social convention to the point that we reject God's will for our lives.

Corporate conscience gives directives in a variety of areas. We do ourselves a favor and avoid heartache when we listen to this conscience. It has our best interest in mind. Looking over the items listed below, we see that each comes with very good reason. We should never be so bold as to assume that we have superior reasoning ability and can ignore this source of help. Space does not permit consideration of each component of our corporate conscience. Some areas it does help us with include
- relationship to God, His name, and His special day;
- relationship to people in the Church and in the world;
- witnessing to our faith in God;
- compassionate concern for others;
- use of our time and money;

- attending public worship services;
- following the Ten Commandments;
- sexual purity;
- marriage and divorce;
- proper care for the body and sanctity of life;
- honesty in business dealings;
- using our tongues wisely;
- being simple and modest in dress and behavior;
- proper use of the media;
- habits and practices of the Christian life.

Each semester in my ethics class, teams of four students present the pro and con arguments of each ethical topic we discuss. Sometimes students will not want to argue a particular position because they spent so much time as a teenager arguing the opposite position with their parents. Their assignment places them on their parents' side, at least for the sake of argument. Most of the time these students will come up to me before their presentation and say, "I can't believe it. I had my mind made up going into the research. I've now come to the conclusion that my parents were right. I'm changing my position." It's always encouraging to see my students mature and grow, and it's also encouraging to learn that their parents are not as out of touch with reality as my students once thought!

Try This

Ask your pastor for a copy of the corporate conscience of your church. Read each item carefully and ask yourself the following questions.
1. What is the biblical basis for this rule?
2. How is it intended to help me in my spiritual life?
3. Am I currently following this rule?
4. If not, what do I need to do to incorporate it into my life?
5. What could be the result if I ignore this rule?

Strategy 21

Get together often to share with and support one another. This strategy follows from the last three. If we see ourselves primarily as members of the Christian community, and if we make ourselves accountable to one another, then it follows that we will want to gather often. We see this practice in the Early Church:

"All the believers were together and had everything in common. Selling their possessions and goods, they gave to anyone as he had need. Every day they continued to meet together in the temple courts. They broke bread in their homes and ate together with glad and sincere hearts, praising God and enjoying the favor of all the people. And the Lord added to their number daily those who were being saved" (Acts 2:44-47).

This is also the reason for the admonition of Heb. 10:25: "Let us not give up meeting together, as some are in the habit of doing, but let us encourage one another—and all the more as you see the Day approaching." Notice the emphasis of encouraging one another in light of Judgment Day.

We gather together as a community of believers not only to worship God and draw closer to Him but also to increase our commitment to the group. That's one of the reasons most Evangelical churches plan several opportunities for believers to get together each week. It is a common characteristic of the development of religious groups.[12] Occasionally I hear the argument that we should schedule only the Sunday morning worship service, since people are busy, and they don't need added responsibility. They can fellowship with God just as well at home. Such arguments miss the point of group bonding. Values, standards, and traditions are mediated to individuals through the group. We really do need that group identity for spiritual encouragement and growth.

Gathering together also provides a social outlet. Much of the social life of Christians should revolve around church activities. The world has so much to offer us that is not spiritually uplifting. Church activities offer a welcomed alternative. An important feature of America's religious history is that the whole town used to turn out for church activities. It was often "the only show in town." Popular culture has changed that. We Christians now have so many options for social outlet. We must guard against the temptation of seeing church activities as just another option. They should be our primary commitment, for that is where our true identity is found.

Try This

Look over the services, Bible studies, age-group meetings, and events scheduled at your church this week.
1. Which ones should you attend?

2. What other activities at school, work, or society present schedule conflicts?

3. Where are your priorities in the event of a conflict? What do those priorities say about your commitment to the Body of Christ?

4. What adjustments do you need to make to your schedule to make your commitment to the Christian community a preference?

Strategy 22

Use your freedom within the Christian community to do good. When Americans are asked to list their highest values, the idea of personal freedom is always at the top of most lists. The Puritans who founded this nation wanted a colony in which they could foster ethical and spiritual life. They saw freedom in the context of liberty to do only good. True freedom was moral freedom to exercise virtue. They formulated the laws of this land around their dream.

We hear a great deal of talk in the public arena today about freedom. Yet what we hear now is a desire to be freed from religious and community constraints. As Robert Bellah and his associates put it in *Habits of the Heart,* "Freedom is perhaps the most resonant, deeply held American value. . . . Yet freedom turns out to mean being left alone by others, not having other people's values, ideas, or styles of life forced upon one." The Puritans never saw freedom as the moral free-for-all that has resulted from cutting it from its religious foundation.[13]

Freedom, like individualism, is a high value among Christians, as it is with the general population. But it's not a freedom to do our own thing even if it's wrong. Paul addressed this matter with the Christians in Galatia: "You, my brothers, were called to be free. But do not use your freedom to indulge the sinful nature; rather, serve one another in love" (5:13). Peter spoke similarly in his first letter to the churches: "Live as free men, but do not use your freedom as a cover-up for evil; live as servants of God" (2:16).

Try This

We hear so often on the news about random acts of violence—freedom used to harm others. Why not use your Christian freedom to do the opposite? How about random acts of kindness?

Think of three things you could do this week to show goodness toward someone.

1.

2.

3.

Strategy 23

Tell your family the Story. One of the most important responsibilities Christian parents have is telling their children God's Story of salvation history. It begins in the Garden of Eden when God promised Adam and Eve a plan of salvation (Gen. 3:15) and continues to this present day in each of our personal lives. The pages of the Bible are filled with the Story; the events of our lives are filled with it as well.

Telling the Story has always been an important task for the people of God. I am impressed with how many times Moses reminded the Hebrew people of this important truth as he gave them his final instructions before they crossed over into the Promised Land. The entire Book of Deuteronomy is that reminder. He said, "It was not your children who saw what he [God] did for you in the desert until you arrived at this place" (11:5). The children would never know about the mighty acts of God in the wilderness wanderings following the Exodus if parents did not set them down and narrate the stories. So Moses gave this instruction: "Impress them on your children. Talk about them when you sit at home and when you walk along the road, when you lie down and when you get up" (6:7). The Story was to become a part of everyday life.

The Hebrew people could not afford to forget. "Only be careful, and watch yourselves closely so that you do not forget the things your eyes have seen or let them slip from your heart as long as you live. Teach them to your children and to their children after them" (4:9). Neither can we afford to forget; we must pass the Story on to our children. Primary responsibility is in the hands of parents; we should not leave the task to a Sunday School teacher or pastor.

So often I hear someone say, "The future is in the hands of our children." This is not really true. The future is and has always been in the hands of God. He has ultimate control of all things. We must tell our children to put their hands in His hand and let Him lead them into the future. That is an important part of the Story. Telling the Story to our children includes giving them good reasons for our ethical beliefs as Christians. When children are very small, we often deny their requests with "Because I said so." But as children grow and develop, they begin to think for themselves. At that point in their development, we must be prepared to provide the supportive defense for our beliefs, based on the Bible and good reason. This will go a long way in helping our children articulate a mature defense for their faith.

Try This

1. If you're a parent, take the opportunity to sit down with your children and tell them your testimony of how you became a Christian. Then review some of the significant events in your life when God worked in miraculous or mighty ways.
2. If you're not a parent, give your testimony and review God's work in your life to a young person in your church. Especially be open to speaking with a child from a single-parent home. Talk with the parent and offer to nurture this child in the Christian faith.
3. Parents might also review their own personal convictions on ethical issues with their children. Children need to know why we believe and act as we do.

Strategy 24

Enjoy the benefit of government acceptance of Christians if you have it; stay true to God and your convictions if you do not have it. United States citizens have heard much talk in the last few decades about the separation of church and state. The discussion came to national attention with the removal of classroom prayer from the public school system in the 1960s. Older baby boomers remember saluting the American flag and having a prayer as every school day began. Younger boomers and generation Xers have only heard about it.

Christians acknowledge that the founding ancestors of this nation created laws for the separation of church and state to keep the state from imposing restrictions on their freedom of worship. In our generation, these laws have been turned on their heads to keep religion out of public life. Pushed to their logical extreme, perverters of church-state laws seek to remove all references to God and faith from public view. For example, a baby boomer student of mine was reprimanded at work for having a small Christmas tree on her desk—one of her coworkers was offended because the tree reminded her of Jesus. My student was ordered to remove the tree or be fired. As a matter of principle, she secured a lawyer and stood her ground. Her employer backed down.

Christians often don't win those church-state battles, however. We're finding ourselves in the minority position more and more; we're also finding that our faith is not respected in society as it once was. In fact, a recent survey indicates that a significant number of people in our society fear Evangelicals. They group us with radicals like the Ku Klux Klan and neo-Nazis and accuse us of trying to impose our personal religious convictions on society. Some even blame us for all the evils in society. We should not despair. Such a change in climate may be good for us and Christ's cause!

Let me explain. Early Christians quickly found themselves at cross-purposes with state government. They faced many local persecutions and two that covered the entire Roman Empire (the persecutions of Nero and Diocletian). Persecutions against Christians ended when Constantine made Christianity an official religion of the empire in A.D. 313 with the Edict of Milan. At that time, Christians who had once been persecuted were then protected. It became socially fashionable to be a Christian. Many church historians believe that state protection was the worst thing that ever happened to the Church. The Church relaxed and became comfortable with the status it enjoyed from the state.

Today the tables have turned. Christians again find themselves out of favor with many state policies. The spiritual climate of surrounding culture is often dark. This may be a golden opportunity for us; it may be our "curtain call" to shine as lights in the spiritual darkness. This could be our shining hour. We should not worry about our lost status with the state, but witness to the power of God.

Try This

1. Look through today's newspaper. Watch for any articles that relate to church-state relations. Notice the arguments of the issue.

2. How might Christians respond to the issue by showing love
   and the right spirit and attitude?
3. Think of three ways the loss of Christian social status might
   help us do a better job of shining as lights in the darkness.
   a.
   b.
   c.

Strategy 25

Gain a renewed emphasis on cultural propriety. Propriety is
knowing what is appropriate in various social circumstances.
This includes the language we use, the subjects we discuss, the
body language we display, and the attitude we portray. We are
receiving such poor models from the media and popular culture
that we can become numb to basic issues of propriety. Television standards have been reduced to whatever can be shown or
said without public outrage, which allows for just about anything. The subjectivism and pluralism of our day tell us that
any language and any topic of conversation is appropriate in
any setting.[14]

I must admit that even as a baby boomer I am stunned at
what I hear from some of my contemporaries and generation
Xers. They will say just about anything about just about anything! God expects better of us. Our corrupt and desensitized
culture gives us no excuse. The word "culture" used to refer to
the highest and the best in social graces. To be cultured meant
that you were socially proper. The thesis of Kenneth Myers's
book *All God's Children and Blue Suede Shoes* is that the wall between high culture and popular culture came down in the
1960s. High culture was characterized by rules and regulations;
popular culture was characterized as a social free-for-all.

Our society opted for popular culture. Now the word "culture" often refers to the worst among us. Television programming is as morally offensive today as the movie industry was a
generation ago. Media and sports celebrities are often not good
role models. Popular music celebrates the dark side of life. We
must not lower ourselves to their level. We must carefully
guard the words that creep into our vocabulary that may be
crude or even vulgar. We cannot afford to be desensitized in this
important area of life. Remember the admonition of Paul in
Eph. 5:4: "Nor should there be obscenity, foolish talk or coarse

joking, which are out of place, but rather thanksgiving." He also reminds us to "avoid godless chatter" (2 Tim. 2:16).

I was speaking to my class about this matter one day when a Christian young woman made a very insightful comment. She said she had gotten angry with her roommate, and before she realized what she was doing, she "cussed her out." She was as shocked as her roommate to hear what had just been said. She immediately asked God and her friend to forgive her. She learned a very important lesson from that experience: it is easy to slip to the level of popular culture. We must guard ourselves and our Christian community against the encroachments of secular society.

Try This

Monitor the conversations you hear on television and among your Christian friends or colleagues for the next week.

1. Name three things you see or hear on television that are crude or ungodly.

   a.

   b.

   c.

2. Name three things that your Christian friends or colleagues say or do that do not reflect cultural propriety for our Christian community.

   a.

   b.

   c.

3. Think of ways you can better monitor your actions and language to keep them consistent with your faith.

Strategy 26

Reaffirm your responsibility to one of the most basic components of the Christian community: family. Before we can let our Christian light shine in the secular world around us, we must be sure it is shining most brightly in our own homes. Christians are sometimes too quick to blame secular society for the loss of a younger generation. Responsibility for the next generation begins with us in our homes. If we do our "homework" well, we can help insulate ourselves against the damaging influences of secular society.

The reason Israel got away from God in the third generation after the Exodus was not due to their pagan environment. Rather, it was because parents did not pass their faith on to their children.[15] Believers have always had to contend with pagan environments. They survived, and so can we. That's why it's so important for us to repeat often and live the Story of salvation in our homes. We must openly discuss among ourselves

- what evils in our world must be avoided;
- why God opposes them;
- practical ways to avoid them;
- the consequences of these evils;
- what Christian virtues should be substituted in their place;
- how our religious faith informs all of our lifestyle choices;
- how to be consistent in our lifestyle witness to the world;
- how to respond if our peers do not respect our choices;
- how to stand alone for what is right.

Success in the Christian home also requires the consistency of avoiding compartmentalizing our lives into secular and sacred realms. We should never be guilty of lifestyle schizophrenia, acting one way at church and another in our home. Family members are amazingly perceptive; they can spot hypocrisy instantly. We owe them a consistent lifestyle that comes from total commitment to God, both in public life and in the home. One of the best compliments you can receive from a family member is the testimony that you live your Christian faith at home.

Try This

1. List three areas in which you can improve your Christian consistency at home.

   a.

   b.

   c.

2. If you have children, sit down with them. Discover areas of moral concern in their lives. Use the discussion starters listed in this strategy to work through some of these concerns with Christian principles and perspectives. Simply talking with your children about these matters will strengthen them spiritually.

Strategy 27

Guard the information flow into your life. Religious history records several occasions in which the church tried to control information flow into the lives of its members. The control of information served two intentions: it was to keep members from becoming curious about what the world had to offer in the way of philosophies and lifestyle choices, and it was to help keep members bonded to the Christian community. The intention was to reduce the influence of the external world.[16] The church sometimes printed lists of books or magazines that were off-limits to its members. Later they frowned on certain forms of secular entertainment, all in the interest of protecting members from the evil influences of society. And rightly so. Bryan Wilson, a sociologist in religion, suggests that religion is always affected when mass media pervades society. It challenges tradition and religious authority.[17] Sometimes the control of information helped protect church members; other times it made them more curious or even rebellious. Ultimately, it was not very successful.

Regardless of how successful it was in the past, external information control will not work in our modern society. Even if the Christian community passed a ban on any usage of television, radio, CDs, computers, magazines, and so on, it could not control everything that comes our way in this information age. That's why the control must be internalized. The motivation to avoid certain things must come from within rather than from without. You must have a solid foundation, both biblically and reasonably, for your personal convictions and make them irreducible minimums for your life.

Let me illustrate. The Internet is now a part of our world. Anyone who has a personal computer can log on and access information anywhere in the world with a few keystrokes. It can be a very beneficial tool. It can also be a conduit of corruption. The Internet can be used to access the worst forms of pornography known to humanity. What should the Christian community do? Should we invent a "Christian chip" to install in all our computers that will not allow access to that information? That won't work. However, we do have some options:

- We can resolve in our own minds that this is not a consistent lifestyle choice for us as Christians.
- We can talk about the problem in our Christian small groups.
- We can talk about the matter to our children.

- We can hold ourselves accountable to one another.
- We can ask the Holy Spirit to keep us sensitive to God's perspective.

In short, we can protect ourselves from the encroachments of the world with an internal motivation that is far more successful than any information control methods that could be imposed from the outside.

Try This

1. Think of three sources of information in your life that you must control as a Christian. They could be the Internet, television, radio, CDs, videos, books, or magazines.

   a.

   b.

   c.

2. Now think of three internal ways you can keep the information flow into your life consistent with your commitment to Christ.

   a.

   b.

   c.

Strategy 28

Incorporate new Christians into your Christian fellowship, and take personal responsibility to disciple them in Christ. Jesus commanded us to evangelize (Matt. 28:19-20). The Book of Acts records the efforts of the Early Church to fulfill that command. The last chapter of Acts ends with more of a comma than a period, indicating that the work must go on in us.

Evangelism has positive results. New people are brought to Christ, and the kingdom of God is enlarged. But evangelism also presents many challenges to the Christian community. One of them is the influence new Christians have on the community. The influence is positive when it brings enthusiasm and new life to the Body; it can be negative if it calls everything into question and we are not prepared to respond. Without care, the net result can be that new Christians influence our lifestyle choices more than we influence theirs. That's why it's essential that we clearly communicate a biblical understanding of our faith and practices. Questions from new Christians can be good when such queries force us to articulate our convictions. We must disciple these new believers in the Word of God and encourage them to seek the Holy Spirit's direction for their lives. God will be faithful to lead them, but we must do our part, not only in evangelism but also in discipleship.

Jesus taught His followers through discipleship. They observed His lifestyle, heard what He said, watched His reactions, and practiced imitating Him through apprenticeship. Jesus' disciples learned from Him much the same way a young craftsman learns from a master. Jesus taught His disciples at three levels:

1. He gave them instruction in the factual information of the faith. This led to the doctrines of the Christian Church.
2. He gave them an education in the way His followers behave in practical, everyday situations. This led to the ethics of the Christian Church.
3. He worked with them in the formation of their character so that they would be believers at the very depth of their beings. This led to the spiritual formation of the Christian Church.[18]

We must do the same as we model our Christian faith to new converts and help assimilate them into the community of faith.

Try This

1. List the five most important features of your faith and lifestyle practice that you feel a new Christian should know.
   a.
   b.
   c.
   d.
   e.
2. Now think of biblical reasons you believe or act this way.
3. If the opportunity presents itself, disciple a new convert into the Christian community. Ask your pastor to help you in any areas in which you are unsure of yourself.

Strategy 29

Revitalize your routine. Routine is a common tendency of all human organizations. Adopting an organization and routine is not bad in and of itself. It is only when such methods are observed with mindless habit that it can be detrimental to our spiritual lives. This tendency is called "institutionalization." Bryan Wilson comments, "There is a tendency for all established and traditional religions to institutionalize their arrangements, and for their activities and relationships to become ossified. This process appears to arise because of an evident tendency of men in all settled cultures to legitimize their procedures by reference to the past."[19]

Richard Niebuhr in *The Kingdom of God in America* writes that the institutionalization of the church begins as an effort to preserve the gains, or conserve the fruit, of a spontaneous or inspirational advancement in the church. Institutionalization may take the form of a two-week revival meeting, conducting Vacation Bible School at 9 A.M., or having a Bible study in the pastor's home. Yet if we are not careful, we will be left with hardened forms and sterile institutions that deny the freedom and spontaneity originally won. God may not need two full weeks of revival services to bring renewal to a congregation; Vacation Bible School might serve a better purpose if it meets in the evening; the Bible study at the pastor's home might run its course and need to be ended. Institutionalization, then, freezes life into forms that, in time, no longer meet our spiritual needs. What started as an aid to faith later becomes a hindrance.[20] It is a hindrance because we are simply going through the motions, form without feeling.

We must constantly be aware of this natural tendency and take measures to keep ourselves from falling into a routine. The way we do this is by continually monitoring our motivation for involvement in community life. We must keep the fervor of our faith alive and realize that participation in the Christian community is a manifestation of that fervor. The desire of a new Christian is to be in church at every opportunity and participate fully in the life of the Christian community. The emotion and enthusiasm are usually replaced in time with a deeper commitment to Christ. But in the process we must never lose our first love, as Christ reminded the church at Ephesus (Rev. 2:4). Our love must ever be for Christ, not a routine.

Try This

1. Review your current involvement in the Christian community.
2. What motivated your involvement in the beginning?

3. Does habit or routine figure into your current motivation?
4. If so, think of measures you can take to recapture your first love.

Strategy 30

In a world looking for a hero, remember the Christian community has the best: Jesus Christ. Every book on the market discussing modern society and popular culture remarks on our loss of true heroes. Popular music tells us we don't need heroes, because none can be found. This hero crisis comes from a number of sources:

- skepticism brought on by false advertising;
- disillusionment created by the moral fall of religious, political, and media celebrities;
- disappointment and frustration brought on by divorce and family separation;
- a loss of belief that it is possible for anyone to be truly virtuous.

Allan Bloom in *The Closing of the American Mind* comes to the conclusion that, since we really do need a hero, our society is urging us to put ourselves on that pedestal and be our own hero. Look up to yourself. This way we don't have to feel uncomfortable with unpleasant comparisons. We are truly free to guide ourselves. But in reality we unconsciously take our cues from the media and sports celebrities of society. "Liberation from the heroic only means that they have no resource whatsoever against conformity to the current 'role models.'"[21]

Those of us in the Christian community have great heroes to admire in the characters of the Bible. Heb. 11 is a hall of fame for faith, naming just a few of the great men and women of the Bible. None of them was perfect in every way, but they do leave us a holy legacy. The Bible does have one hero, however, who was perfect in every way. Jesus Christ is a role model and a hero for all time. He was and is the Man for all seasons. Christians need not suffer the hero crisis of our secular society. Society has done everything in its power through the ages to discredit our Hero. It always has and always will fail in its attempts.

So when you need a hero, follow the advice of the writer of Hebrews: "Let us fix our eyes on Jesus, the author and perfecter of our faith" (12:2). He will never let you down!

Try This

1. Why do we need heroes?
2. Think of popular heroes in society who have fallen from their pedestals. What caused them to fall?
3. Think of ways the world has tried to discredit Jesus Christ as a hero.
4. Why do these attempts to discredit Jesus always fail?
5. List five qualities of Jesus that you would like to develop in your own life.

   a.

   b.

   c.

   d.

   e.

9

Line 'em Up: Part 3

*Strategies for Your Relationship
with the World*

Strategy 31

Live your life in the world but not of it. Jesus gave us this strategy in John 17:16-18. Let's break this phrase apart and analyze it. First, we are to live *in* the world. That is, we are to live our lives in the flow of society. We work and play with the world all around us; we interact with it. Second, we are *not* to live *of* the world. That is, we are not to adopt the world's value system or worldview. We insulate our minds against the contaminating influences of the way the world thinks and processes reality. Our affections and desires are not the same as the world's. The world does not set the agenda for the way we live our lives.

However, we must not be anticulture. That would be counterproductive. Jesus had no strategy of isolating His followers into a separate subculture away from the general public. Some groups of Christians through the ages have sought to do this as a way of avoiding the evil influences of the world. They withdrew into mountains, forests, or deserts to create a separate environment totally isolated from society. Jesus taught, rather, that we are to be salt and light and yeast in our society (Matt. 5:13-14; 13:33). Salt has to be poured out of the shaker. Light must go into the darkness. Yeast must be worked into the lump of dough. In other words, we Christians must live and work in the world to be an influence for good on it. But we must maintain our separate and distinct identity in thinking and in lifestyle choices.

Try This

1. Using Jesus as your Model, think of ways He illustrated with His life the principle of living your life in this world but not of it.
   a. In what ways did Jesus participate in the normal flow of life?
   b. In what ways did He avoid the world's way of thinking?
2. Examine your own life.
   a. In what ways do you participate in the normal flow of life?
   b. In what ways do you avoid the world's way of thinking?

Strategy 32

Share your faith whenever appropriate. We should follow the advice of Peter when he said, "Always be prepared to give an answer to everyone who asks you to give the reason for the hope that you have" (1 Pet. 3:15). This does not mean you must preach on the street corner, but it does mean you are always ready with a good report of what the Lord has done for you whenever the opportunity presents itself.

One of my favorite examples of a simple report of God's work comes from Jesus' healing of a man born blind. Jesus angered the Pharisees by healing on the Sabbath day. They brought the healed man in and interrogated him. Then they interrogated his parents. Finally they reinterrogated the healed man. During his second interrogation, the Pharisees tried to sidetrack him in a complicated theological debate. The healed man cut through the complications and simply testified to what Jesus had done for him: "Whether he is a sinner or not, I don't know. One thing I do know. I was blind but now I see!" (John 9:25).

Society is hungering as never before for answers to life's questions. This is a great time to offer Christ as the Answer for the deepest needs of life. Some scientists and technology specialists promised they could meet all our needs—they would eliminate evil through greater knowledge and improved lifestyle. They tried to paint God out of the picture, telling us that religious faith has no relation to life, that the natural order is all there is, that we can depend only on ourselves, that God talk is meaningless.

This generation of baby boomers and Xers has realized the bankruptcy of these hollow promises. Scientists and technologists have not delivered us from evil. As Robert Bellah put it, science has delivered us into the abyss.[1] Look at events around the world. Political systems are failing. Economic systems are not working very well. Social systems are in crisis. This has created a spiritual hunger in our generation.[2] We know the answer: Christ. Declare it unashamedly every chance you get.

Try This

1. Write out the answers to life's questions that God has provided for your life.
2. Compare your life before you were a Christian to now. Note the differences.
3. Be prepared to share your findings with a non-Christian friend or colleague. You don't have to preach to him or her. Just report what God has done for you.
4. Urge your friend or colleague to try God on a trial basis.
5. Support your friend or colleague with prayer and encouragement if he or she takes you up on your offer.

Strategy 33

Look to the early Christian church for guidance and support. We sometimes feel we're facing a world that is far more corrupt and hostile than any previous generation has ever faced. This is not true. God and the Church have always had their enemies. You are in good company. Jesus himself said, "If the world hates you, keep in mind that it hated me first" (John 15:18). Jesus faced hostility throughout His ministry; the apostle Paul faced the same hostility as he spread the gospel through the pagan Gentile Roman Empire. Issues and battle strategies have changed across the years, but the underlying hatred of the Christian message is the same.

As we look at church history, we see that the Early Church not only survived but flourished in the midst of cultural, social, and religious diversity. They too faced pluralism, relativism, subjectivism, humanism, and paganism. They understood the strategy of living in the world but not of it. They actually could have enjoyed protection under Roman law as a private group. But they chose instead to live with their culture and be an influence for good (salt, light, and yeast). When their society began to disintegrate under the weight of its own moral bankruptcy, they were present and ready to confront it with the claims of the gospel message. They even helped rebuild their society on a solid biblical foundation.[3]

History is again repeating itself. We are faced with many of the same social and cultural conditions that surrounded the Early Church. We must follow the example of our ancestors and confront our culture on its own ground. Those who fought the good fight of faith and have gone on to heaven are now there cheering us on to victory. They form the "great cloud of witnesses" spoken of in Heb. 12:1. We owe God and them our best effort. We are following in a great tradition and have a great heritage to uphold.

Try This

1. Think of three ways our popular culture is like the pagan cultures of Paul's time. For starters read Acts 12:21-23; 14:8-20; 17:16-34; 19:23-41; 1 Cor. 5:1-2; 8:1-13.

   a.

   b.

   c.

2. Think of three ways Christians can be positive witnesses and role models to people in our culture.

   a.

   b.

   c.

3. What responsibility do we have to the "great cloud of witnesses" who have given us the heritage of our faith?

Strategy 34

Stay in touch with culture. We must be aware of the direction of popular culture without getting sucked into its influence. A wise military strategist always knows the enemy's position. How can we wisely counter culture's errors if we don't know what they are? You do not have to participate in the world's evil practices to be aware of them. For example, I don't attend movie theaters. But I do read movie reviews and stay in touch with what Hollywood is producing. I also occasionally listen to the Top 40 countdown on the radio. I read up on cultural trends and watch for developments through entertainment industry programs and magazines. In this way I can carry on an intelligently informed conversation with my friends and coworkers who are in the culture battle. It is hard for us to relate to our world if we do not remain current.

Christians sometimes do a disservice to the cause of righteousness by engaging in conversation with a non-Christian only to present incorrect or outdated information. Walt Mueller calls this "the egg-on-the-face syndrome."[4] This causes the world to believe that we are out of touch or ignorant of modern life. We must do our homework if we are going to be good representatives for Christ's cause.

This strategy must be kept in perspective, however. It can become a full-time job and divert us from more important tasks! We must also guard against becoming desensitized to the evils of culture. Awareness must never breed complacency. Some entertainment magazines have sections called "What's Hot and What's Not." Read those occasionally. The list changes weekly. Entertainers and trends are in constant flux. A hit song this week may be off the charts next week. Hollywood's hottest stars often fade quickly. That's why I have specifically avoided referring to entertainers, television shows, movies, or music artists by name. It's possible that they could be out of the limelight before this book goes to print. So remember: you don't have to be on top of every new music group and every movie produced, but you should stay in touch.

Try This

Just for fun, test your knowledge of popular culture in the following areas. Check with just about any teenager for the correct answer if you don't know.

1. What are the three most popular television programs this season?
2. Who is *People* magazine's most popular male and female this year?
3. What are the three hottest rock bands?
4. Who is currently the best rapper?
5. Who has the most popular talk show on television?
6. Who is at the top of the country music charts?
7. Who received the Academy Award for best actor? actress?
8. What is the most popular line of slogan T-shirts?
9. What is the latest buzzword from popular culture?
10. Who is the highest-paid celebrity in Hollywood? How much does he or she make?

How did you do? Are you in touch with popular culture? If you aren't, don't feel too deprived—you're not missing much!

Strategy 35

Remember that your true citizenship is in heaven. Paul reminds us of this in Phil. 3:20. We actually have dual citizenship. We carry a passport or a driver's license identifying us as a citizen of a certain country and state. But we also have our names written in the Lamb's Book of Life (Rev. 13:8; 21:27), granting us eternal life, which began the moment we accepted Christ as our Savior. We are citizens of earth and heaven at the same time.

Occasionally a student comes to our university with dual citizenship. He or she enjoys the privileges of both countries. Dual citizens travel freely in either country. However, most of them prefer to call one of these countries "home." In that same way, Christians live, work, and play as citizens of this earth. All the while, we never lose sight of the fact that this world is not our final residence. We are just passing through on our way home. We are always a bit uncomfortable and have a deep, inner longing to be with our Lord. We keep a light touch on the things of this world. Paul reminds us in 1 Cor. 7:31 that we may "use the things of the world," but we should not become "engrossed in them. For this world in its present form is passing away."

Stanley Hauerwas and William Willimon explore this concept in their book *Resident Aliens.* They discuss our privileges and responsibilities as members of the Christian colony on this earth: "The church was called to be a colony, an alternative community, a sign, a signal to the world that Christ had made possible a way of life together unlike anything the world had seen."[5] When we become a Christian, we join a journey that began long before we got here and will continue long after we are gone.[6] In the Sermon on the Mount Jesus gives us instructions for living in this colony (Matt. 5—7). He draws the distinctions plainly between the world and the colony. The authors comment:

> Here is an invitation to a way that strikes hard against what the world already knows, what the world defines as good behavior, what makes sense to everybody. The Sermon, by its announcement and its demands, makes necessary the formation of a colony, not because disciples are those who have a need to be different, but because the Sermon, if believed and lived, makes us different, shows us the world to be alien, an odd place where what makes sense to everybody else is revealed to be opposed to what God is doing among us.[7]

The authors go on to say that the admonitions of the Sermon on the Mount are far more than instructions on how to live in the colony. Rather, they are a picture of the way God is—how He thinks, how He responds. Too often we place the focus of the sermon on us and our behavior rather than on God and His nature. When we learn who God is, we then know how we should live in order to please Him. Lifestyle choices made in the colony are important, because we are setting our affections and preparing our soul for eternity in heaven.

Try This

1. Think of the last time you were away from home for a week or more. List three evidences that you did not plan to stay away from home permanently.

   a.

   b.

   c.

2. Now think of three evidences of your lifestyle or patterns of thought that indicate that this earth is not your final home.

   a.

   b.

   c.

Strategy 36

Live as a counterculture. If we're going to be in the world but not of it, we must decide on a strategy for positioning ourselves in relationship to our society. We have already shown that Jesus does not want us to withdraw and adopt a monastic lifestyle. Withdrawal removes our godly influence from the world. Neither does He want us to blend in so that we live and think like the world; this has been the stance of many mainline Protestant denominations for the past several years. What alternative is left? We can be a counterculture.

Our call to be salt, light, and yeast is a call to challenge the incorrect beliefs and corrupt practices of our age. We must point out the absurdity, the folly, the outright sin of it all.[8] We must be proactive, taking the offensive in seeking to permeate secular society with the ideals and realities of Christian culture. Rather than just condemning culture, we offer a workable alternative to it. We challenge the notion that life can be complete and fulfilling without God and His plan. We model our talk in our personal lives, our homes, and our churches. We live life based on God's truth, objective standards of right and wrong, and biblical principles. We point out the bankruptcy of the world's positions and offer alternatives that are rich with meaning and fulfillment.

"The most creative social strategy we have to offer is the church. Here we show the world a manner of life the world can never achieve through social coercion or governmental action."[9] We show the world how a life, a family, a group of people look and act when God is working in their midst. We should be the best advertisement God has for promoting His ways. Reginald Bibby reminds us that in the language of consumer society we have an extremely marketable product.[10] It is a product that provides wholeness and satisfaction in life. Withdraw from the world? Never. We have a responsibility to help reconnect God and people in secular society.

Try This

1. Think of three social problems that business, science, technology, and government have not been able to solve, for which Christ has an answer that works.

   a.

   b.

   c.

2. What is the best way Christ can get His answer to the needy people of His world?

Strategy 37

Maintain the priority between your primary and secondary cultures. This strategy is a logical conclusion of the last two—having heavenly citizenship and living as a counterculture. Our primary culture is the Christian community, the colony of heaven; our secondary culture is the world in which we live. Two important processes maintain this priority—enculturation and acculturation.

Enculturation happens both formally and informally as we bring children and new Christians into the community of faith. They learn to live, talk, and think like Christians. Acculturation happens as believers learn to accommodate themselves to their surrounding culture and function in it, while at the same time maintaining their primary identity as a member of the Christian community.

It is a practical reality that Christians can be enculturated into the Christian community and acculturated to function in the world without compromising the fundamentals of their faith. However, this happens successfully in a pluralistic society only when a conscious effort is made to distinguish between the two cultures and to set priorities as to which one is going to be primary. The obvious problem, which we have discussed extensively in this book, is that we Christians are receiving mixed signals every day. Culture can kill us softly. We hear one thing when we go to church and read our Bibles, and we hear quite another when we live in the world. Christian citizens of a counterculture, who live and work in a larger worldly culture, always run the risk of getting turned around. We can become comfortable as members of the larger society and view our membership in an institutional church as just another social obligation. We are aware of the risk and fight it with efforts to remain supremely loyal to Christ and aliens in the larger society.[11]

Try This

Think of distinguishing ways a Christian should think or act in the following areas.
1. Celebration of Christmas and Easter
2. Use of language
3. Use of leisure time
4. Manner of dress
5. Driving habits
6. Treatment of enemies
7. Use of money
8. Selection of close friends
9. Treatment of authority figures
10. Use of Sunday

Strategy 38

Recognize that the world processes reality differently today than it did in the past. We are too close to the transition to have a clear perspective on it, but philosophers who study these matters characterize it as a move from "modern" to "postmodern" thinking. Only time will tell if this assessment is correct. Regardless of the final outcome, the current discussion offers helpful insights into differences in the way people think today when compared to the past. To understand this transition, note three terms:
1. *Premodern.* This is an acceptance of traditional authority in

religion and the church with a high value placed on a unified voice in thinking and society. In this mode of thought, one listens to the church.

2. *Modern.* Here authority shifts from religion to science but does not destroy a somewhat unified voice in thinking and society; knowledge is certain and objective. In this mode of thought, one listens to science.

3. *Postmodern.* The search for unity is abandoned, leaving a disjointed collection of styles and interpretations. No claim to universality is made; knowledge is uncertain and subjective. Truth is fragmented into a thousand pieces to be defined by a thousand individuals. No boundaries are left to define anything. In this mode of thought, one listens to no source in particular.[12]

This helps explain why our society encourages religious pluralism and rejects the authority of the Bible, the objectivity of truth, and the concept of universal norms, all of which come from premodern thought. The philosophical spirit of this age argues against everything for which Christians stand. Realizing and accepting this fact will go a long way in helping us coexist in a world that thinks very differently from the way we think as Christians. Actually, we are operating on a different wavelength than the world.

Because many baby boomers and most of generation X have been raised in this philosophical spirit, we must watch for its influences in our Christian lives and attempt to bring our thinking processes in line with the biblical perspective. That is, we must constantly remind ourselves of the authority of the Bible, the objectivity of truth, and the concept of universal norms. Awareness of the situation is nine-tenths of the battle.

Many times I have returned home from sharing my faith with an unchristian friend and felt as though I was out of touch with reality. I honestly feel sometimes as if I'm in a philosophical twilight zone. The subjectivity and relativism of our day is enough to make us want to quit even trying to relate the gospel message to postmoderns. But God has called us to live and proclaim the message. The Holy Spirit empowers us. He will see to the harvest—the victory is His.

Try This

1. Think of an example of the premodern way of thinking.

2. Think of an example of the modern way of thinking.
3. Think of an example of the postmodern way of thinking.
4. What is the best strategy to use in witnessing to a friend or coworker who thinks as a postmodern?

Strategy 39

Constantly remind yourself that you are not immune to the contaminating influences of secular culture. We encounter the philosophies of this world on a daily basis. We must recognize their presence and subtle influences and guard against their traps.

One of the most important ways we do this is through a regular regimen of resensitivity. It is easy to slip into a condition of insensitivity. A poster I use in my ethics class shows a married couple enjoying an evening in their family room. The man is watching a sexy television program while also looking through the swimsuit edition of his latest sports magazine. The woman is reading a soap opera digest to catch up on the most recent gossip from her daytime dramas. The caption at the bottom of the poster reads, "How much do we have to see before we go blind?"

Our constant exposure to the philosophies of this age (relativism, pluralism, egoism, hedonism, determinism, secular humanism, and nihilism) can blind us to their effects. In time these effects appear to be normal; we become insensitive to their deadly impact. Let me illustrate. My wife and my mother are both great cooks, and I have enjoyed good cooking most of my life; however, my first year of seminary was a glaring exception. I was on my own and not very skilled in the kitchen. So I fixed a lot of instant potatoes and boxes of macaroni and cheese that year. I ate so many plates of instant potatoes, in fact, that I actually forgot how real potatoes tasted. After Sue and I married, she served a bowl of real mashed potatoes. I didn't like them; I thought something was wrong with them. My taste buds preferred the artificial to the real thing!

The same thing can happen to our thinking. That's why we must periodically stop and take inventory of what philosophies are being advocated and what effect they are having on us.

Our son, Brent, had an assignment in public school a couple of years ago that required him not to watch television for two weeks. That's a difficult assignment for a generation Xer! He actually went through a bit of media withdrawal. But the assignment was good for him and his parents. When he turned the television back on, he had new eyes and ears with which to evaluate cultural influences. He was surprised at how much he saw and heard. Paul reminds us in Rom. 12:2, "Do not conform any longer to the pattern of this world, but be transformed by the renewing of your mind. Then you will be able to test and approve what God's will is—his good, pleasing and perfect will."

Try This

1. Try Brent's assignment. Leave the television off for two weeks. When you turn it back on, notice what you see and hear to which you had grown immune.
2. Put your mental antenna up, and listen for all the philosophical messages coming subtly from culture. Keep a piece of paper with you for two weeks, and write them down every time you encounter them.
3. After you complete the first two exercises, make a list of all the secular influences against which you need to guard yourself.

Strategy 40

Recognize the proper place of entertainment in the whole scheme of life. In chapter 6 we looked at 1 Cor. 10:23—11:1 under the heading "Consider Others." Let's look at that same passage from another perspective at this point in the discussion. Paul says it's not a problem for Christians to eat meat that has been offered to idols as long as they realize the consecration has no true spiritual reality. In other words, Christians must not buy into the philosophy of the pagan myth. Kenneth Myers compares Paul's meat reference to popular culture. It is not wrong for Christians to be entertained by popular culture so long as we keep our lives focused on objective reality and don't participate in things that violate our Christian convictions. We refuse to buy into the subjectivism, materialism, hedonism, and all other operative philosophies of our society. We are in trouble when we allow our culture to define reality for us.[13]

Consider the following suggestions to help keep secular entertainment in its proper place and control its influence on your life and home.

1. Protect yourself from media addiction.

2. Avoid the extreme of attempting to cut yourself off from all media influences; that is an unrealistic expectation and will only lead to frustration.
3. Learn how to discern the harmful from the harmless and how to use good judgment in rejecting all that is displeasing to God.
4. Don't allow entertainment to become a divisive element in your home by disrupting mealtime, separating family members into different rooms to view different programs on television, arguing over what to watch or hear, sacrificing family unity, and creating rebellion over forbidden programs.
5. Set boundaries of acceptable programs and time limits, both personal and family, and stick to them.
6. Ask the Holy Spirit to give you wisdom in controlling entertainment's influence.[14]

Try This

1. List all of the various ways you can spend your personal and family leisure time.
2. Now prioritize the list according to what you personally spend the most time doing. Note where entertainment falls on your list.
3. Take measures to place entertainment in its proper place, as one option in life among many. Establish guidelines to keep it there.

Strategy 41

Shift the discussion from "rights" to "what is right." Dropping the last letter in the word "rights" makes a world of difference. The discussion in the public arena regarding rights is occurring in every area of life. You can hardly watch a newscast without hearing individuals or groups demanding their rights. A random sample newscast carried two such stories. One dealt with a national movement to protect homosexuals under laws designed to prevent discrimination against minority groups; the other dealt with a debate in the United States Congress to allow women to have a particular abortion procedure until the day of delivery. Both news stories focused attention on the rights of these people to be protected by national law to do what they want.

Our problem is in discussing these issues with the wrong language. From a Christian perspective, the issue is not about rights; it is about what is objectively right or wrong. Practices that are morally wrong do not deserve national protection. Dallas Willard, professor of philosophy at the University of Southern California, offers the following analogy: Are you discriminating against a couple if you refuse to rent your apartment to them because they have been legally removed from the last three residences for vandalism and nonpayment of rent? Are you discriminating against individuals for not allowing them to baby-sit your children when they have recently been convicted as child molesters?[15] Certainly not. These are not issues of *rights*—they relate to what is *right*.

The discussion about rights breaks down when the behavior or lifestyle is immoral. Morality, of course, implies universal norms, truth, God, and all the other Christian principles we have discussed. Our society has drifted into the discussion of rights because it has lost touch with what is right. Take immoral sexual practices, for example. "Those who engage in such sexual behavior . . . want to be explicitly recognized as morally on a par with everyone else. And if you refuse to recognize them, you will very likely be morally attacked as a bigot and as someone opposed to tolerance, pluralism, and cultural inclusivism."[16]

These public discussions seldom include God's perspective on the matter. As Christians we must have the spiritual insight to judge an action according to the Word of God. If it is biblically defined as immoral, we have a responsibility to shift the discussion from rights back to what is *right*. Remember, no human redefining of moral actions changes God's will or the consequences. Regardless of how politically incorrect we are accused of being, we dare not compromise the truth of God.

Try This

1. Watch the news for current discussions by individuals or groups regarding their rights. Examine the matter from God's perspective.
2. In these particular cases, is there a need to shift the discussion from rights to what is right?
3. How should Christians respond to the matter?

Strategy 42

Strengthen your defense against the world's influences through value inoculation. We are familiar with the concept of inoculation in the medical field. Our bodies are strengthened to defend themselves against a certain virus by being exposed to a mild case of the virus. Strategy 7 emphasized taking inventory of your personal convictions and knowing what you believe and why; strategy 34 urged you to stay in touch with culture. Strategy 42 goes a step farther in preparing refutations for each of the world's positions. Value inoculation argues in favor of the positions of the world and requires us to create counterarguments. We sometimes call this strategy "playing the devil's advocate." It is a very good tool to use in any small-group setting of Christians.

I use this strategy often in my ethics class. We will be involved in a discussion of a certain ethical issue, and students will be defending their position. Without telling them what I am doing, I throw some value inoculation into the debate; that is, I argue the world's position. For example, I argue that Anglo Christians have a right to be prejudiced toward minorities, because this is our country, and they are trying to take it away from us; we must protect what is ours. I can tell by the look of shock and horror in their eyes that some of my students have never prepared a counterargument to this position. They are totally thrown off-balance by my remarks. My purpose is to help them regain their balance on more solid ground.

Two cautions are necessary when using this strategy. First, adults can easily overpower the fragile moral philosophy of most teenagers and some young adults. The purpose is not to destroy their belief system; it is to help them critically analyze and develop their belief system until it is intellectually and spiritually strong and stable. Second, keep your feet firmly planted in Christian truth as you consider the world's views. Don't get disoriented in the fog of the relative chaos of secular humanism. We don't help the cause of Christ when we leave believers confused and uncertain of their beliefs.[17]

Try This

Use value inoculation in a small group of which you're a member. If you're not the leader, discuss your plan with the group leader ahead of time to explain what you're doing and why. Don't end the discussion until it is resolved in favor of the Christian position. Finally, explain value inoculation to the group so they understand the motive and the value of what you've just done.

Strategy 43

In your interaction with the world, emphasize the positive rather than the negative side of Christian ethical positions. The world often has a very negative stereotypical view of Christians. They describe us as dressing, working, and living with utmost seriousness; we never have fun, and we certainly never smile. One author titled an article about a Christian group, "Where the Lord Usually Said, NO." Last week one of my baby boomer students raised his hand in an ethical discussion and asked, "If you guys don't smoke, and you don't drink, and you don't gamble, don't you have any fun in life?" Unfortunately, that's the misperception by too many people in our world about Christians. We must seek to change that image.

Truthfully, the Christian position is not primarily a negative one. That is, it is not what we stand against in the world that matters to us. Rather, it is what we positively stand for that we must emphasize. To emphasize the things we don't do, say, wear, or buy is to misunderstand the motivation of Christian lifestyle choices. We don't simply delete the issues we find objectionable and remain in a vacuum. We live in another, more positive realm. This is what helps characterize us as citizens of the heavenly colony. We have left the world behind in pursuit of a higher goal. It is a different lifestyle based on a different value system.

The Christian lifestyle can be both satisfying and enjoyable. And, yes, as I answered my student, Christians laugh and have fun. In fact, I would argue that Christians get more out of life than non-Christians. We don't deal with the hangovers or nausea associated with social drinking. We don't have to worry about getting social diseases associated with lax sexual practices. We don't expose our bodies to diseases associated with smoking or drinking. We don't worry about the devastating results of experiencing an adulterous affair or business fraud. We don't live with the haunting guilt that comes from a variety of sinful practices. We don't experience the emptiness and lack of fulfillment that comes from living out of fellowship with God. We have been freed to enjoy life on earth to the fullest extent.

Try This

Review some of your lifestyle choices. Compare them with the opposite choices your non-Christian friends or coworkers make. Answer the following questions.
1. Why do you choose not to live as your friends or coworkers live?
2. What advantages do your choices have over their choices?
3. What heartaches and problems are you avoiding with your choices?
4. What positive virtues are being built into your life by your choices?
5. Do you feel the Christian lifestyle is superior in the long run to the non-Christian lifestyle? Why?

Strategy 44

Make sure your accommodations to the world are translations — not transformations. Our world is constantly changing; Christians must change with it. However, we must always be on our guard that the changes we make in our beliefs or practices are updates or translations of our heritage and don't transform it into something different. Updating in and of itself is not bad; we must update our methods and structures to remain relevant to our society. The process that transforms our faith into something different is called "secularization" by sociologists of religion. It is the process in which too little tension exists between the religious institution and the world; the former is conquered by the latter and surrenders to its standards.[18]

The translation of our faith to a new generation is not secularization. Some people don't make this important distinctive, so they judge all change in the church as worldly accommodation. Milton Yinger, a sociologist of religion, points out, "What is often called secularization today is the inevitable adjustment of the church to dramatic changes in the world within which it works."[19] The ability of a church to update itself and stay in step with the times is a sign of strength, rather than a sign of weakness. Such updating may be in the form of a more contemporary worship style or using a variety of instruments during corporate singing. It may require changing service times or inviting people to dress more casually for Sunday evening services. Examples follow below. A church that remains static becomes locked into a particular mode of operation and fails to answer the questions of a new generation with the life-changing message of Christ.

We must accommodate our faith, practices, methods, and structures to the changing needs of our culture. However, we must keep our feet firmly planted in the biblical foundation of our faith in order to be able to distinguish between the essentials and the nonessentials as we attempt to translate our faith. God the Holy Spirit can help us do this without transforming our religion into something different.

Try This

1. Look over the following list of things Christians believe and do. Place an *E* after things you consider essential; place an *NE* after things you consider nonessential.
   a. Sunday morning order of worship
   b. The Bible as primary Authority for matters of faith and practice
   c. Vacation Bible School meeting weekdays from 9 A.M. until 12 Noon
   d. Justification by grace through faith
   e. A Bible study group meeting every Thursday night in our home
   f. Taking the Lord's Supper as a community of believers
   g. Particular hairstyles
   h. Worshiping together
   You should recognize the essentials above as *b*, *d*, *f*, and *h*, and the nonessentials as *a*, *c*, *e*, and *g*.
2. What is the overall quality of the essentials? of the nonessentials?
3. Now that you see the difference between essentials and nonessentials, think about other things Christians believe and do. Distinguish the essentials. Ask your pastor about questions you have regarding particular ones.
4. Think of three principles we can use as we change with our society without being transformed into something different.
   a.
   b.
   c.

Strategy 45

Above all, your relationship with the world should be marked by love. Jesus taught us about love in the Sermon on the Mount when He told us to love our enemies. Reread that message in Matt. 5:43-48. It is easy to be kind to those who are nice to us; it is not that easy to have that same regard for those who mistreat us. But that's the revolutionary charge Jesus gave us. In fact, the concept of love is one of the most important features of the Christian faith. The Bible contains more than 500 verses that talk to us about it.

God never tells us to do something that He himself does not do. God is the very essence of love, and He expects His disciples to bear that characteristic. In fact, Jesus says we demonstrate that we are like God by loving our enemies.

I was terribly offended by a television scene I saw last week. It showed a group of proclaiming Christians who were protesting homosexuality. One of the protesters carried a large sign that read, God Hates Queers. Nothing could be farther from the truth. God does not hate any human being, regardless of a sinful lifestyle. He despises the sinful act, but He loves the individual and seeks to bring him or her back to himself. Jesus gives us a clear example of this when He witnessed to the Samaritan woman at the well (John 4:4-26). Although He knew that she was living immorally, that did not stop Him from loving her and trying to help her.

Earlier in the book we noted what an incredible risk God took in giving humanity a free will. It was entirely possible that we might use our free will to disobey Him. God took another incredible risk in His plan with humanity: to a large extent He put His reputation in our hands! That idea amazes me. When people look at the way we apply the gospel message to our lives, they draw conclusions about God. They believe about His love what they see us demonstrate toward them. That's an awesome responsibility that requires the help of the Holy Spirit on a daily basis. Such love does not come naturally from within; it is the gift of God that flows through us. We become a channel He uses to reach His world in love. That's why He placed us on earth; that's the task He gave us to complete.

This last strategy brings us full circle in our Christian ethic. We have vital fellowship with God because He first loved us. Now we accept His love for ourselves and pass it on to everyone in our world. Jesus reminds us, "By this all men will know that you are my disciples, if you love one another" (John

13:35). We started our strategies with God's love, and we end with it.

Try This

Think of five individuals in your world whom God can love through you. Write down their names and ways you can love them in the days ahead.

1.
2.
3.
4.
5.

10

Wrapping Up

Where Is Our Hope?

"On Second Thought" Revisited

I began this book by describing my encounter with the young woman who told me in class that her personal entertainment choices did not matter. I honestly felt like quitting my job that day, because I sensed that popular culture had won the battle. But I had second thoughts and decided to stay at the task. Why? Because the battle with our culture is not over, and Christians have not surrendered. I admit that popular culture has had a profound impact on all of us, especially generation Xers and baby boomers. It has impacted us not only in what we say and do but, more importantly, in the way we think. It is killing us softly in ways we may not even realize.

The time has arrived for those of us who take the name of Christ to wake up and talk about this matter one-on-one, in small groups, and from our pulpits. It will be of great benefit for us simply to sit down and talk together about the influences and impact of our world on our Christian thinking and lifestyle. I know that not everything you read in this book was new to you. You've probably heard some of it often in your life. Nevertheless, it's good for us to review it, to think it through again, and to talk about its implications for our lives.

---

1. Our hope is in talking together and acting on our new insights.

There Is Hope

There is hope! That's why I didn't quit my job. That has been the sole intent of this book—to communicate hope. Yes, there is hope as long as we are willing to consider these matters openly. Once we have them at the center of our thinking, the Holy Spirit can work with us in fresh ways to keep Kingdom priorities first. I see change in the lives of my generation X and baby boomer students every semester. Quite often a student will come to me at the end of an ethical discussion and say, "Our discussion got through to me. I've changed my position on this matter." A mother of one of my students sent me this note: "I don't know what happened in ethics class, but it changed the course of my daughter's life. Thanks." Occasionally students will report that they went home or to their dorm rooms after class and cleaned up their CD or videocassette collection so that it would be consistent with their Christian commitment. Several students have told me they now change the television channel when the language or plot violates Christian principles.

2. Our hope is in forming a counterculture.

Half Empty or Half Full

Optimists are often characterized as seeing a glass half full, while pessimists see it as half empty. Our mind-set of optimism or pessimism will go a long way in determining where we go in the battle with culture. The pessimistic approach throws up its hands in defeat. It either gives up on culture and withdraws from society, taking an anticulture approach to life, or it gives in to culture and blends with society, embracing all that culture has to offer. The optimistic, hopeful approach, on the other hand, lives in society but takes the approach of a counterculture. We challenge our world on its own terms with a Christian approach to life. We don't have any grandiose plans of creating a perfect society with our efforts, but we're confident that we can have a significant impact for Christ on our generation.

3. Our hope is in realizing that society is changing and that we must change with it.

Not Business as Usual

We must realize that things are not as they've always been in our society. In the last three decades our society has changed more than at any other time in our history. We must acknowledge this change and confront it. We Christians must not bury our heads in the sand and refuse to admit that everything around us is changing. George Barna identifies the 1990s as "the pivotal decade in the history of American Christianity."[1] This period is so crucial because society is changing so rapidly. We will either adapt to these radical changes, or we'll find ourselves in one of two conditions:

1. overpowered by the world's influence;
2. out of touch with our world and unable to relate the claims of the gospel to it.

4. Our hope is in facing the uncertain challenge together.

A Spirit of Uncertainty

All of this change has brought a spirit of uncertainty to our national life. Robert Bellah and his associates state, "Perhaps most common today is a note of uncertainty, not a desire to turn back to the past but an anxiety about where we seem to be headed."[2] Uncertainty has resulted because the change has occurred slowly. We refer to sudden change as a revolution; the cultural changes of the 1960s were a revolution. Revolutions make the news and get our attention. Slow change is an evolution; it occurs almost unnoticed. Yet slow changes can be just as powerful. They change "our values, beliefs, perspectives, lifestyles, institutions, and ways of doing things."[3]

Our society has moved from something fixed to something uncertain. The challenge for Christians is to keep our moral and cultural bearings in this uncertain world. The need for Christians to be *in* the world has never been greater; the way to avoid being *of* the world has never been more difficult. Again, talking together about this challenge and brainstorming ways to remain victorious will help us.

Satan has a better chance of defeating me if he can isolate me and make me feel that I'm the only one facing this challenge. We can foil his effort simply by sharing our struggles and our victories with one another. When a friend tells me he has turned off a television program or canceled a magazine subscription or convinced his local convenience store not to carry pornography, I know I'm not alone in the culture war and am encouraged to do better with my own efforts. When I admit to others that I'm growing weary in the culture battle, I'm in a position to have my Christian brothers and sisters boost me with encouragement.

---

5. Our hope is in taking our stand for God's truth.

Stand Up and Be Counted

Another encouraging feature for Christians in the culture war is a willingness among us to "stand up and be counted." Researchers of baby boomers and generation Xers agree that both generations are more willing than ever to commit themselves to a noble cause. Baby boomers in the 1990s are reaching midlife and are reevaluating their priorities, redefining their values, and reflecting on the purpose and significance of life. They are realizing that material possessions and self-fulfillment efforts do not satisfy. They are open and ready to commit themselves to something that does satisfy. They are also facing their own mortality and renewing their interest in spiritual matters.[4]

The same openness to commitment is seen in generation Xers. While skeptical of much the world has to offer, they are ready to stand up and be counted if they can be convinced the cause is true. Volunteerism and commitment to worthy causes is at an all-time high among generation Xers.[5] My current students quickly respond to calls for involvement in ministry-related service and in taking social and ethical positions. Hope for the cause of Christ is bright because boomers and Xers are more willing than ever to take their stand for what is true and right. With that resolve, God's Spirit can work among us to build His kingdom in people's lives.

---

6. Our hope is in God's way, which works.

It Works

Another encouraging note among Christians is the evidence that our faith makes us better citizens of this earth and offers better solutions to the problems of life. That was the clear conclusion of the research of Patterson and Kim in their book *The Day America Told the Truth:* "Religion appears to play a strong role in building moral character. We found that people who defined themselves as religious showed a much stronger commitment to moral values and social institutions than did nonreligious people."[6] Religious people are more willing to die for what they believe. They are more sure of their own moral worth. They are at peace with themselves. They are more satisfied with their lives, less likely to use illegal drugs, more committed to family, better workers, and less prone to petty crime.[7]

The Christian way also offers better solutions to social problems. A recent evening news report dealt with a religiously based drug rehabilitation program. The program focuses on biblical principles and God as the Source of help through faith in Jesus Christ. It operates on a modest budget without federal or state funding. Best of all, it's highly successful. Seventy percent of the graduates of the program remain drug-free after they leave.

Officials of the state-funded programs admit that they cannot even approximate these figures. Their drug rehabilitation programs are much more expensive, funded entirely with taxpayers' money. They use licensed counselors who are trained in religious-free techniques that produce only modest results. The best success figures for graduates are under 25 percent.

It sounds as though the state would want to partner with the first program, right? Wrong! The state is trying to revoke their license to exist and shut them down for minor problems like torn shower curtains. And why? Because they refuse to use the state's religion-free counseling techniques—techniques that the state admits don't work! A Princeton University research professor who has studied the matter said that without question God and religious faith are the reason for the phenomenal results and are the only hope for drug addiction.

---

7. Our hope is in remembering that the battle is the Lord's.

Reluctant to Listen

The previous illustration points not only to the workability of the Christian position but also to society's reluctance to acknowledge God's truth. As Kenneth Myers puts it, "Living in a culture that is increasingly hostile to Christian living is one of the most consistent trials we will face."[8] Our current situation is as challenging as the persecutions and plagues of the early Christians.[9] Our Christian ancestors didn't flee from the challenge, and neither can we. Here again we will find strength for the battle by talking about it together and strategizing our battle plan.

Jesus warned us during His earthly ministry that the worldly mind-set does not accept the ways of God. Read this assessment again in John 15:18—16:4. Especially focus your attention on 15:20: "Remember the words I spoke to you: 'No servant is greater than his master.' If they persecuted me, they will persecute you also. If they obeyed my teaching, they will obey yours also." When I become weary in the attacks against my Christian positions, I remember that people are not attacking me personally; they are attacking God and His truth. As Jesus reminded us, "They will treat you this way because of my name" (v. 21). I am greatly encouraged when I know our fight is for the cause of Christ.

---

8. Our hope is in God!

The Ultimate Strategy

Not only must we remember that the battle is the Lord's,

but also we must recall that our strength comes from Him. It is very helpful for us to get together and support one another and to strategize battle plans for the fight. Ultimately, however, our victory comes from the empowerment of the Holy Spirit, who lives and works in our lives. As the prophet Zechariah assessed the situation, it is "'not by might nor by power, but by my Spirit,' says the LORD Almighty" (4:6). All the strategies and moral resolve in the world cannot help us unless the Spirit of God is working within us. With His help we are sure to win.

When I think of the reasons for my hopefulness concerning the culture battles and our place in them, I believe this is the greatest reason of all: God has called us into battle. He has promised to go before us and to walk beside us. He gives us all we need to take our stand for Him. We know from reading the Bible that victory is certain. Perhaps the greatest privilege of the Christian life is that we have God at our side. We have already read the last chapter of the book, and God wins. So keep hope high and fight on, Christian pilgrim—you are on the winning team. "Now to the King eternal, immortal, invisible, the only God, be honor and glory for ever and ever. Amen" (1 Tim. 1:17).

LIST OF STRATEGIES

1. Begin by checking to *see that your relationship with God is where it should be.*

2. *Take inventory to be sure that you are approaching life with a Christian worldview.*

3. *Hear all that God has to say.*

4. *Focus your eyes to see the spiritual reality of life.*

5. *Saturate your life with the Word of God.*

6. *Break down the wall in your thinking between secular and sacred.*

7. *Take inventory of your personal convictions on ethical issues; know where you stand, based on the Bible and good reason, and refuse to compromise.*

8. *Carefully guard what you allow your mind to dwell upon.*

9. *Control the flow.*

10. *Analyze the return on your investment.*

11. *Look past the surface messages of media to the deeper agenda being presented.*

12. *Consider the consequences.*

13. *Train your conscience.*

14. *Keep temptation in perspective.*

15. *Remember in your ethical decision-making that you are preparing your soul for eternity.*

16. *See your individualism in the context of the larger Christian community.*

17. *Remember that as a member of the Christian community, you are not alone.*

18. *Make yourself accountable to the Christian community.*

19. *Maintain your connection to community tradition.*

20. *Submit yourself to the corporate conscience of the Christian community.*

21. *Get together often to share with and support one another.*

22. *Use your freedom within the Christian community to do good.*

23. *Tell your family the Story.*

24. *Enjoy the benefit of government acceptance of Christians if you have it; stay true to God and your convictions if you do not have it.*

25. *Gain a renewed emphasis on cultural propriety.*

26. *Reaffirm our responsibility to one of the most basic components of the Christian community: family.*

27. *Guard the information flow into your life.*

28. *Incorporate new Christians into your Christian fellowship, and take personal responsibility to disciple them in Christ.*

29. *Revitalize your routine.*

30. *In a world looking for a hero, remember the Christian community has the best: Jesus Christ.*

31. *Live your life in the world but not of it.*

32. *Share your faith whenever appropriate.*

33. *Look to the early Christian church for guidance and support.*

34. *Stay in touch with culture.*

35. *Remember that your true citizenship is in heaven.*

36. *Live as a counterculture.*

37. *Maintain the priority between your primary and secondary cultures.*

38. *Recognize that the world processes reality differently today than it did in the past.*

39. *Constantly remind yourself that you are not immune to the contaminating influences of secular culture.*

40. *Recognize the proper place of entertainment in the whole scheme of life.*

41. *Shift the discussion from "rights" to "what is right."*

42. *Strengthen your defense against the world's influences through value inoculation.*

43. *In your interaction with the world, emphasize the positive rather than the negative side of Christian ethical positions.*

44. *Make sure your accommodations to the world are translations — not transformations.*

45. *Above all, your relationship with the world should be marked by love.*

NOTES

Chapter 1

1. Gary R. Collins and Timothy E. Clinton, *Baby Boomer Blues* (Dallas: Word Publishing, 1992), 4-6.

2. Ibid., 6.

3. Ibid., 17.

4. James Bell, *Bridge over Troubled Water: Ministry to Baby Boomers—a Generation Adrift* (Wheaton, Ill.: Victor Books, 1993), 19.

5. Daniel Yankelovich, *New Rules: Searching for Self-fulfillment in a World Turned Upside Down* (Toronto: Bantam Books, 1981), 7.

6. Ibid., 10.

7. Andrés Tapia, "Reaching the First Post-Christian Generation," *Christianity Today*, September 12, 1994, 19.

8. Ibid.

9. James Patterson and Peter Kim, *The Day America Told the Truth: What People Really Believe About Everything That Really Matters* (New York: Prentice Hall, 1991), 218.

10. William Mahedy and Janet Bernardi, *A Generation Alone* (Downers Grove, Ill.: InterVarsity Press, 1994), 23.

11. Ibid., 30.

12. Ibid., 25.

13. Ibid., 28.

14. Robert Frost, "The Road Not Taken," in *Literature: An Introduction to Reading and Writing*, ed. Edgar V. Roberts and Henry E. Jacobs (Englewood Cliffs, N.J.: Prentice Hall, 1989), 885-86.

Chapter 2

1. Josh McDowell and Bob Hostetler, *Right from Wrong* (Dallas: Word Publishing, 1994), 6; and Tapia, "Reaching the First Post-Christian Generation," 19.

2. Yankelovich, *New Rules*, 89.

3. Ibid., 262-64.

4. Robert N. Bellah et al., *Habits of the Heart* (New York: Harper and Row, Publishers, 1985), 43.

5. McDowell and Hostetler, *Right from Wrong*, 257-58.

6. Nancy Tatom Ammerman and Wade Clark Roof, *Work, Family, and Religion in Contemporary Society* (New York: Routledge, 1995), 62-64.

7. Yankelovich, *New Rules*, 97.

8. Patterson and Kim, *The Day America Told the Truth*, 6.

9. Ibid., 25.

10. Ibid., 25-26.

11. Ibid., 27.

12. Ibid., 45-46.

13. Ibid., 49.
14. Ibid., 73, 89.
15. Ibid., 71, 83.
16. Ibid., 73.
17. Ibid., 80.
18. Ibid., 7.
19. Ibid., 81.
20. Ibid., 8, 89.
21. Ibid., 90.
22. Ibid., 88.
23. Ibid., 94-95.
24. Mahedy and Bernardi, *A Generation Alone*, 99.
25. Patterson and Kim, *The Day America Told the Truth*, 96-97.
26. Ibid., 95.
27. Ibid., 170.
28. Ibid., 173.
29. Ibid., 7.
30. Ibid., 8, 120.
31. Ibid., 155.
32. Ibid., 156-57.
33. Ibid., 215.
34. Ibid., 65.
35. Ibid., 7.
36. Ibid., 171-72.
37. Ibid., 201.
38. Ibid., 199-200.
39. Ibid.
40. Ibid., 203.
41. Bellah et al., *Habits of the Heart*, 63.
42. Patterson and Kim, *The Day America Told the Truth*, 204.

Chapter 3

1. Herbert Schlossberg, *Idols for Destruction: Christian Faith and Its Confrontation with American Society* (Nashville: Thomas Nelson Publishers, 1983), 8.
2. Ibid., 144.
3. Ibid., 7.
4. Burton F. Porter, *Reasons for Living* (New York: Macmillan Publishing Co., 1988), 4-5.
5. Bell, *Bridge over Troubled Water*, 53.
6. Patterson and Kim, *The Day America Told the Truth*, 102-3.
7. Bryan R. Wilson, "Religious Toleration and Religious Diversity" (Santa Barbara, Calif.: Institute for the Study of American Religion, 1995), 42.
8. Ayn Rand, *For the New Intellectual* (New York: Penguin Books USA, 1961), 65.
9. Ayn Rand, *The Virtue of Selfishness* (New York: Penguin Books USA, 1964), x.
10. Ibid., 66-67.
11. Schlossberg, *Idols for Destruction*, 166-67.
12. Porter, *Reasons for Living*, 109-10.

13. Patterson and Kim, *The Day America Told the Truth*, 142.

14. Ibid., 216.

15. Yankelovich, *New Rules*, 83-84.

16. Schlossberg, *Idols for Destruction*, 41-42.

17. Ibid., 58.

18. Paul Kurtz, ed., *Humanist Manifesto II*, (Buffalo, N.Y.: Prometheus Books, 1973), 16.

19. Ibid., 18.

20. To this discussion we might add secularism, utopianism, Marxism, scientific humanism, naturalism, rationalism, or existentialism.

Chapter 4

1. William B. Coker, "Tradition," in *Beacon Dictionary of Theology*, ed. Richard S. Taylor (Kansas City: Beacon Hill Press of Kansas City, 1983), 525.

2. Walt Mueller, *Understanding Today's Youth Culture* (Wheaton, Ill.: Tyndale House Publishers, 1994), 67.

3. William J. Bennett, *The De-Valuing of America: The Fight for Our Culture and Our Children* (New York: Summit Books, 1992), 25.

4. Kenneth A. Myers, *All God's Children and Blue Suede Shoes* (Wheaton, Ill.: Crossway Books, 1989), 34.

5. Allan Bloom, *The Closing of the American Mind* (New York: Simon and Schuster, 1987), 187, 197.

6. Myers, *All God's Children and Blue Suede Shoes*, 40-42.

7. Ibid., 31.

8. Bennett, *The De-Valuing of America*, 34.

9. Myers, *All God's Children and Blue Suede Shoes*, xiii.

10. Bennett, *The De-Valuing of America*, 25.

11. Ibid., 26.

12. Myers, *All God's Children and Blue Suede Shoes*, 27.

13. Ibid., 28.

14. Ibid., 59-61.

15. Mueller, *Understanding Today's Youth Culture*, 78.

16. Tapia, "Reaching the First Post-Christian Generation," 22.

17. Mueller, *Understanding Today's Youth Culture*, 126.

18. Ibid., 78-79.

19. McDowell and Hostetler, *Right from Wrong*, 5.

20. Ibid., 12.

21. Patterson and Kim, *The Day America Told the Truth*, 26.

22. Ibid., 3.

23. Ibid., 8.

24. McDowell and Hostetler, *Right from Wrong*, 7.

25. Ibid., 15-16.

26. Bloom, *The Closing of the American Mind*, 25.

27. Ibid., 60.

Chapter 5

1. Reginald W. Bibby, *Fragmented Gods* (Toronto: Stoddart Publishing Co., 1987), 1-2.

2. A. W. Tozer, *The Knowledge of the Holy: The Attributes of God: Their Meaning in the Christian Life* (New York: Harper and Brothers, Publishers, 1961), 7, 10.

3. Ibid., 112.

4. Norman L. Geisler, *Christian Ethics: Options and Issues* (Grand Rapids: Baker Book House, 1989), 17-22.

5. Roland Bainton, *Here I Stand: A Life of Martin Luther* (New York: Abingdon-Cokesbury Press, 1950), 183-85.

Chapter 7

1. Stephen V. Monsma, "Christian Worldview in Academia," *Faculty Dialogue* 21 (spring-summer 1994): 140-42.

2. Bibby, *Fragmented Gods*, 233.

3. Bert Hodges, "Faith-Learning Integration: Appreciating the Integrity of a Shop-Worn Phrase," *Faculty Dialogue* 22 (fall 1994): 95-106.

4. Myers, *All God's Children and Blue Suede Shoes*, 160.

5. Ibid., 66, 83-85.

6. A good source of information on this subject for generation X is Mueller, *Understanding Today's Youth Culture*. A good source for baby boomers is Michael Medved, *Hollywood vs. America: Popular Culture and the War on Traditional Values* (New York: HarperCollins Publishers, 1992).

7. Mueller, *Understanding Today's Youth Culture*, 158-61.

8. Ibid., 163-64.

9. Bloom, *The Closing of the American Mind*, 228.

10. Adapted from Lauriston J. DuBois, *Guidelines for Conduct* (Kansas City: Beacon Hill Press, 1965), 42-47.

11. Adapted from Milton L. Rudnick, *Christian Ethics for Today: An Evangelical Approach* (Grand Rapids: Baker Book House, 1979), 135-48.

Chapter 8

1. Bellah et al., *Habits of the Heart*, 37.

2. Ibid.

3. Ibid., 223.

4. Ibid., 143.

5. Mahedy and Bernardi, *A Generation Alone*, 30.

6. Bellah et al., *Habits of the Heart*, 77.

7. Ibid., 97.

8. Patterson and Kim, *The Day America Told the Truth*, 40.

9. Bellah et al., *Habits of the Heart*, 65.

10. Stanley Hauerwas and William H. Willimon, *Resident Aliens* (Nashville: Abingdon Press, 1989), 72.

11. Ibid., 97.

12. Bryan R. Wilson, "An Analysis of Sect Development," *American Sociological Review* 24 (February 1959): 14.

13. Ibid., 23, 29.

14. Myers, *All God's Children and Blue Suede Shoes*, 99.

15. McDowell and Hostetler, *Right from Wrong*, 47.

16. J. Alan Winter, *Continuities in the Sociology of Religion: Creed, Congregation, and Community* (New York: Harper and Row, Publishers, 1977), 159-60.

17. Bryan Wilson, *Religion in Sociological Perspective* (New York: Oxford University Press, 1982), 129.

18. John Westerhoff, "Fashioning Christians in Our Day," *Faculty Dialogue* 17 (spring 1992): 9-14.

19. Wilson, *Religion in Sociological Perspective,* 121.

20. Richard Niebuhr, *The Kingdom of God in America* (New York: Harper and Row, Publishers, 1937), 164-69.

21. Bloom, *The Closing of the American Mind,* 66-67.

Chapter 9

1. Bellah et al., *Habits of the Heart,* 277.

2. Mahedy and Bernardi, *A Generation Alone,* 40-42; and Schlossberg, *Idols for Destruction,* 146.

3. Westerhoff, "Fashioning Christians in Our Day," 23-24.

4. Mueller, *Understanding Today's Youth Culture,* 169.

5. Hauerwas and Willimon, *Resident Aliens,* 132.

6. Ibid., 52.

7. Ibid., 74.

8. Myers, *All God's Children and Blue Suede Shoes,* 32.

9. Hauerwas and Willimon, *Resident Aliens,* 83.

10. Bibby, *Fragmented Gods,* 261.

11. Westerhoff, "Fashioning Christians in Our Day," 12-14.

12. Howard Ozmon and Samuel Craver, *Philosophical Foundations of Education,* 5th ed. (Englewood Cliffs, N.J.: Prentice Hall, 1995), 362-63.

13. Myers, *All God's Children and Blue Suede Shoes,* 87.

14. Some of these steps are adapted from Mueller, *Understanding Today's Youth Culture,* 164-68.

15. Dallas Willard, "No Pluralism in Moral Matters?" *Discernment,* winter 1994, 2.

16. Ibid.

17. James Waller, "The Case Against Value Indoctrination in Higher Education," *Faculty Dialogue* 19 (winter 1993): 65-76.

18. J. Milton Yinger, *Sociology Looks at Religion* (London: Macmillan Publishers, 1961), 69-71.

19. Ibid., 71-72.

Chapter 10

1. Quoted in Collins and Clinton, *Baby Boomer Blues,* 99.

2. Bellah et al., *Habits of the Heart,* 276.

3. Collins and Clinton, *Baby Boomer Blues,* 99.

4. Bell, *Bridge over Troubled Water,* 29, 31; and Patterson and Kim, *The Day America Told the Truth,* 29.

5. Tapia, "Reaching the First Post-Christian Generation," 19; and Mahedy and Bernardi, *A Generation Alone,* 83, 125-28.

6. Patterson and Kim, *The Day America Told the Truth,* 61.

7. Ibid., 202.

8. Myers, *All God's Children and Blue Suede Shoes,* 34.

9. Ibid., xii.

BIBLIOGRAPHY

Primary Books

Ammerman, Nancy Tatom, and Wade Clark Roof. *Work, Family, and Religion in Contemporary Society.* New York: Routledge, 1995.

Bainton, Roland. *Here I Stand: A Life of Martin Luther.* New York: Abingdon-Cokesbury Press, 1950.

Bell, James. *Bridge over Troubled Water: Ministry to Baby Boomers—a Generation Adrift.* Wheaton, Ill.: Victor Books, 1993.

Bellah, Robert N., Richard Madsen, William M. Sullivan, Ann Swidler, and Steven M. Tipton. *Habits of the Heart.* New York: Harper and Row, Publishers, 1985.

Bennett, William J. *The De-Valuing of America: The Fight for Our Culture and Our Children.* New York: Summit Books, 1992.

Bibby, Reginald W. *Fragmented Gods.* Toronto: Stoddart Publishing Co., 1987.

Bloom, Allan. *The Closing of the American Mind.* New York: Simon and Schuster, 1987.

Collins, Gary R., and Timothy E. Clinton. *Baby Boomer Blues.* Dallas: Word Publishing, 1992.

DuBois, Lauriston J. *Guidelines for Conduct.* Kansas City: Beacon Hill Press, 1965.

Geisler, Norman L. *Christian Ethics: Options and Issues.* Grand Rapids: Baker Book House, 1989.

Hauerwas, Stanley, and William H. Willimon. *Resident Aliens.* Nashville: Abingdon Press, 1989.

Kurtz, Paul, ed. *Humanist Manifesto II.* Buffalo, N.Y.: Prometheus Books, 1973.

Lewis, Hunter. *A Question of Values: Six Ways We Make the Personal Choices That Shape Our Lives.* San Francisco: Harper and Row, Publishers, 1990.

Mahedy, William, and Janet Bernardi. *A Generation Alone.* Downers Grove, Ill.: InterVarsity Press, 1994.

Maston, T. B. *Biblical Ethics.* Waco, Tex.: Word Books, 1967.

McDowell, Josh, and Bob Hostetler. *Right from Wrong.* Dallas: Word Publishing, 1994.

Mueller, Walt. *Understanding Today's Youth Culture.* Wheaton, Ill.: Tyndale House Publishers, 1994.

Myers, Kenneth A. *All God's Children and Blue Suede Shoes.* Wheaton, Ill.: Crossway Books, 1989.

Niebuhr, Richard. *The Kingdom of God in America.* New York: Harper and Row, Publishers, 1937.

Ozmon, Howard, and Samuel Craver. *Philosophical Foundations of Education.* 5th ed. Englewood Cliffs, N.J.: Prentice Hall, 1995.

Patterson, James, and Peter Kim. *The Day America Told the Truth: What People Really Believe About Everything That Really Matters.* New York: Prentice Hall, 1991.

Porter, Burton F. *Reasons for Living.* New York: Macmillan Publishing Co., 1988.

Rand, Ayn. *For the New Intellectual.* New York: Penguin Books USA, 1961.

———. *The Virtue of Selfishness.* New York: Penguin Books USA, 1964.

Roberts, Edgar V., and Henry E. Jacobs, eds. *Literature: An Introduction to Reading and Writing.* Englewood Cliffs, N.J.: Prentice Hall, 1989.

Rudnick, Milton L. *Christian Ethics for Today: An Evangelical Approach.* Grand Rapids: Baker Book House, 1979.

Schlossberg, Herbert. *Idols for Destruction: Christian Faith and Its Confrontation with American Society.* Nashville: Thomas Nelson Publishers, 1983.

Tozer, A. W. *The Knowledge of the Holy: The Attributes of God: Their Meaning in the Christian Life.* New York: Harper and Brothers, Publishers, 1961.

Wilson, Bryan. *Religion in Sociological Perspective.* New York: Oxford University Press, 1982.

Winter, J. Alan. *Continuities in the Sociology of Religion: Creed, Congregation, and Community.* New York: Harper and Row, Publishers, 1977.

Yankelovich, Daniel. *New Rules: Searching for Self-fulfillment in a World Turned Upside Down.* Toronto: Bantam Books, 1981.

Yinger, J. Milton. *Sociology Looks at Religion.* London: Macmillan Publishers, 1961.

Journal and Magazine Articles

Hodges, Bert. "Faith-Learning Integration: Appreciating the Integrity of a Shop-Worn Phrase." *Faculty Dialogue* 22 (fall 1994): 95-106.

Monsma, Stephen V. "Christian Worldview in Academia." *Faculty Dialogue* 21 (spring-summer 1994): 139-47.

Tapia, Andrés. "Reaching the First Post-Christian Generation." *Christianity Today,* September 12, 1994, 18-23.

Waller, James. "The Case Against Value Indoctrination in Higher Education." *Faculty Dialogue* 19 (winter 1993): 65-76.

Westerhoff, John. "Fashioning Christians in Our Day." *Faculty Dialogue* 17 (spring 1992): 5-25.

Willard, Dallas. "No Pluralism in Moral Matters?" *Discernment* (winter 1994): 2, 6.

Wilson, Bryan R. "An Analysis of Sect Development." *American Sociological Review* 24 (February 1959): 3-15.

———. "Religious Toleration and Religious Diversity." Santa Barbara, Calif.: Institute for the Study of American Religion, 1995.

FOR FURTHER READING

On Ministry to Baby Boomers

Bell, James. *Bridge over Troubled Water: Ministry to Baby Boomers—a Generation Adrift.* Wheaton, Ill.: Victor Books, 1993.

Collins, Gary R., and Timothy E. Clinton. *Baby Boomer Blues.* Dallas: Word Publishing, 1992.

On Ministry to Generation Xers

Mahedy, William, and Janet Bernardi. *A Generation Alone.* Downers Grove, Ill.: InterVarsity Press, 1994.

On Christians Living in Secular Culture

Bennett, William J. *The De-Valuing of America: The Fight for Our Culture and Our Children.* New York: Summit Books, 1992.

Bloom, Allan. *The Closing of the American Mind.* New York: Simon and Schuster, 1987.

Hauerwas, Stanley, and William H. Willimon. *Resident Aliens.* Nashville: Abingdon Press, 1989.

Medved, Michael. *Hollywood vs. America: Popular Culture and the War on Traditional Values.* New York: HarperCollins Publishers, 1992.

Mueller, Walt. *Understanding Today's Youth Culture.* Wheaton, Ill.: Tyndale House Publishers, 1994.

Myers, Kenneth A. *All God's Children and Blue Suede Shoes.* Wheaton, Ill.: Crossway Books, 1989.

Schlossberg, Herbert. *Idols for Destruction: Christian Faith and Its Confrontation with American Society.* Nashville: Thomas Nelson Publishers, 1983.

On Objective Truth

McDowell, Josh, and Bob Hostetler. *Right from Wrong.* Dallas: Word Publishing, 1994.

On a General Christian Ethic

Geisler, Norman L. *Christian Ethics: Options and Issues.* Grand Rapids: Baker Book House, 1989.

On Cultural Beliefs

Mitchell, Susan. *The Official Guide to American Attitudes: Who Thinks What About the Issues That Shape Our Lives.* Ithaca, N.Y.: New Strategist Publications, 1996.

Patterson, James, and Peter Kim. *The Day America Told the Truth: What People Really Believe About Everything That Really Matters.* New York: Prentice Hall, 1991.